MW00617280

Day Hiking the
North Georgia Mountains

Day Hiking the
North Georgia Mountains

Jim Parham

**milestone
press**

an imprint of the
University of Georgia Press
Athens

Published by Milestone Press,
an imprint of the University of Georgia Press
Athens, Georgia 30602
www.ugapress.org
© 2012 by Jim Parham
All rights reserved
Book design by Jim Parham
Book design by Denise Gibson/Design Den www.designden.com
& Jim Parham
Cover photographs by Jim Parham (front) & Mary Ellen Hammond (back).
All interior photographs are by the author unless otherwise indicated.

Library of Congress Cataloging-in-Publication Data

Parham, Jim.
    Day hiking the north Georgia mountains / Jim Parham.
      p. cm.
    ISBN 978-1-889596-26-6 (alk. paper)
    1. Hiking—Georgia—Guidebooks. 2. Mountains—Georgia—
Guidebooks. 3. Georgia—Guidebooks. I. Title.
    GV199.42.G46P37 2012
    796.5109758—dc23
                        2011052656

Printed digitally

This book is sold with the understanding that the author and
publisher assume no legal responsibility for the completeness
or accuracy of the contents of this book, nor for any damages
incurred while attempting any of the activities or visiting any
of the destinations described within it. The text is based on
information available at the time of publication.

THE APPALACHIAN TRAIL HEADS NORTH FROM HORSEBONE GAP

Table of Contents

Introduction 10

Hiking Guidelines
Gear Checklist 12
Clothing & Fitness 13

Safety
Getting to the Trailhead 14
On the Trail 15
Things to Look Out For 16

How To Use this Book 20

Northeast Georgia

Three Forks Trail 24
Holcomb Creek Trail 27
Rabun Bald Trail 30
Pinnacle Knob View 33
Tennessee Rock Trail 36
J.E. Edmonds Trail 39
Whiteoak Stomp View 42
Hemlock Falls Trail 45
Tallulah Gorge Circuit 48
Panther Creek Trail 51
Chenocetah Mountain 54
Nancytown Falls 57

Eastern Blue Ridge

Miller Trek 62
Arkaquah Trail 65
Brasstown Bald Summit 68
Wagon Train Trail 71
Wolfpen Ridge 74
Chattahoochee Source 77
High Shoals Trail 80
Tray Mountain Summit 83
Rocky Mountain Loop 86
Mount Yonah Trail 89
Dukes Creek Falls Trail 92
Raven Cliffs Trail 95
Whitley Gap Shelter 98
Cowrock Mountain View 101
Bear Hair Gap Trail 104
Coosa Backcountry Trail 107
Slaughter Creek Loop 110
Blood Mountain Loop 113
Levelland Mountain View 116
Desoto Falls Trail 119

Dahlonega

Atlanta

Eastern Blue Ridge

Table of Contents (cont.)

Western Blue Ridge

Dockery Lake Trail 124
Preaching Rock View 127
Woody Gap Ramble 130
Sassafras Mountain View 133
Brawley Mountain Firetower.. 136
Deadennen Mountain View .. 139
Wallalah Mountain View 142
Toccoa River Bridge 145
Rich Mountain Loop 148
Long Creek Falls 151
Springer Mountain Loop...... 154
Amicalola Falls Loop 157
AT Approach Loop............. 160
Wildcat Creek Trail 163

Cohutta Mountains

Jacks River Falls 168
Rice Camp Loop................. 171
Panther Creek Falls............. 174
Grassy Mountain Tower 177
Little Bald Mountain View 180
Panther Bluff View 183
Fowler Mountain View 186
Emery Creek Trail.............. 189
Stone Tower Loop 192
Cools Springs Loop............. 195
West Face Loop 198

Northwest Georgia

West Rim Loop.................. 204
Sittons Gulch Trail 207
Zahnd Natural Area............210
High Point Loop.................. 213
Rocktown Loop..................... 216
Taylors Ridge Trail............... 219
Johns Mountain Loop.......... 222
House of Dreams Loop 225

Appendices

Appendix A—Resources Contact Information 230
Appendix B—Summit Bagging in North Georgia 233
Appendix C—Hike Routes in State Parks..................................... 234
Appendix D—Hike Routes on the Appalachian Trail..................... 234
Appendix E—Hike Routes on the Bartram Trail 235
Appendix F—Hike Routes on the Benton MacKaye Trail................ 235
Appendix G—Hike Routes with Waterfalls 235

Introduction

Day hiking in the north Georgia mountains is one of the best ways to see, *really see*, what this beautiful region has to offer. Here is where mountains rise to well over 4,000 feet, where Georgia's mightiest rivers are born, where striking cliffs offer panoramic views, where waterfalls crash in secluded coves, where wildflowers bloom, where white-tailed deer and black bear and ruffed grouse roam, and where the very air tastes clean and fresh. On a trail, on foot, time slows down. There are no deadlines to meet, no traffic to dodge; it's just you and the woods. You can walk all day or for just an hour. In no time, the demands of everyday life fade away, and the forest comes alive. It's peaceful, energizing, and exhilarating.

The north Georgia mountains mark the southern end of the Appalachian chain, which runs the length of the eastern seaboard, all the way up through Maine and into Newfoundland. In Georgia they stretch from the east near Clayton to the west atop Lookout Mountain; the highest peak is Brasstown Bald at 4,784 feet. Right in the middle of Georgia's share of the Appalachians is Chattahoochee National Forest, boasting six state parks and numerous other tracts of land managed by the Georgia Department of Natural Resources. Foot trails found on these publicly owned lands are numerous, well marked, and well maintained. Some, like the Appalachian Trail with its southern terminus atop Springer Mountain, are world famous.

This book describes 65 hiking routes. Rather than covering every inch of every trail in the region, its purpose is to bring you the best day hiking options. Each hike has at least one destination. It might be a scenic view from a high summit. It might be a secluded waterfall. You might climb over a narrow gap or to a stone lookout tower. You might hike past a waterfall, up a mountain to multiple scenic views, and then through a rugged gorge. Every route is different, and each one has that extra something to make it more than just a walk in the woods.

When is the best time to go for a hike? That's a common, easily answered question. The best time to go is when you *can* go. The important thing is to be prepared for what the season may bring, and then choose your hike accordingly. The information accompanying each route in this book will help you make that decision. Spring, summer, fall, and winter each have their own characteristics, and any of them can be a great time to get out on the trail.

Spring is when the woods come alive. Green shoots sprout up from the forest floor, and at times it seems that every plant is in bloom. Hikers seem to walk with an extra spring in their step at this time of the year. The new growth, the warm sun, and the fresh air make you feel good all over.

As the spring transitions to summer, the woods take on a different feel. Plants grow lush, and the once expansive views close in as the leaves fill out on the trees. Afternoons begin to feel hot and sultry. It's as if everything—you, the plants, the ground, the air—is sweating. Hikes during the height of summer should be planned near cool streams or early in the day, before things heat up. Carry extra water in your daypack.

Just when you think that if it gets any hotter or drier the whole of north Georgia will catch on fire, the season turns again. With the cooler weather and lower humidity of fall, the air clears up. Sometime in October the tree leaves begin to change color. For two or three weeks, entire mountainsides will be ablaze with red, yellow, purple, and rusty orange hues. Eventually they'll go brown and fall to the ground, and you'll hike along through great piles of them crackling under your feet.

Winter comes to north Georgia in fits and starts. Some days are sunny with temperatures into the sixties, while others are dark and dreary with bone-chilling cold. Short-lived snowstorms can be numerous or nonexistent, depending on the year. This is not the season to put away your hiking shoes. Instead, pull on a couple of extra layers and hit the trail. Temperatures can be ideal for hiking at this time of year, and on clear days, you can see forever.

So, if you want to see, *really see*, the best of north Georgia, lace up your boots, grab your day pack, head up into the mountains, and strike out on the trail.

Hiking Guidelines

Gear Checklist

Nothing can ruin a good hike quicker than leaving something essential behind. Remember the scout motto? Be prepared. Here's a checklist of items for a day hike.

Footwear
- comfortable hiking boots or shoes
- woolen or synthetic socks that fit well (no cotton)

Outerwear (be prepared to add layers; no cotton shirts or jeans)
- shorts or light pants and quick-dry t-shirt (this is your base layer)
- cap or wide-brimmed hat

In Your Daypack
- lunch/high-energy snacks
- water (2 liters per person)
- insect repellent
- personal first-aid kit
- sunscreen and lip balm
- rain jacket (always)
- long-sleeved shirt (always)
- emergency flashlight
- map and/or guidebook
- small plastic trash bag

Nice To Have
- walking stick or trekking poles
- pocket knife or multi-tool
- camera

Clothing & Fitness

Dress for the weather. The key word to remember is layers. The weather in the north Georgia mountains can be very fickle. A day that starts out with abundant sunshine and warm temperatures can quickly turn to a cold fog or a sudden thunderstorm. No matter what the forecast, be prepared with multiple layers. A rain jacket over a long-sleeved shirt over a short-sleeved shirt, with a hat to top it off, will keep you warm in most conditions. If you're hot, take something off. If you're cold, put more on. And remember, leave your cotton at home.

What about that footwear? Day hiking requires a choice of footwear different from what you need for serious backpacking. You may relish the idea of purchasing a pair of stiff, rugged, hiking boots, but in reality they are not necessary and may even tire you out sooner. Lightweight hiking boots or shoes, or even trail runners are perfectly adequate for a day hike. Choose supportive footwear that fits well. Too tight or too loose a fit will cause blisters and jammed toenails—definitely something you don't want. If your route includes numerous stream crossings (a few of the hikes in this book do), make sure you wear something you don't mind getting wet. It's much easier, safer, and quicker to just walk on through a creek with your shoes on than taking them off and trying to tiptoe across slippery underwater rocks barefooted.

Assess your fitness level. All the hikes in this book can be accomplished in a day or less, sometimes much less. The approximate hiking time listed for every hike assumes an average level of hiking fitness. Attempting an all-day hike "right off the couch" is not recommended. Before heading into the woods, assess your fitness level and choose a hike that matches what you honestly think you can accomplish in the time you have available.

Safety

Getting to the Trailhead

For many of the hikes in this book, getting to the trailhead is no big deal. All of Georgia's state parks and many of its recreation areas have well-maintained paved roads and parking lots. However, there are also quite a few trailheads that can be reached only by traveling on unimproved roads. Driving a vehicle on a winding, rocky, steep mountain road is significantly different from traveling on smooth asphalt. Even if you are accustomed to gravel roads, it's a good idea to take things slowly and be extra careful. Here are some driving tips to ensure a safe and enjoyable experience.

- First of all, slow down—*really* slow down. A vehicle does not respond the same way on loose stones and dirt as it does on a paved surface. Too much speed and you'll drift dangerously to the outside of curves, where safe braking becomes impossible. Remember, the idea is to enjoy the scenery, not make time.
- While driving, keep your eyes on the road. If you want to look at a view, stop the car in the middle of the road if you need to (as long as you're not on a blind curve) and take a look. Chances are no one is behind you, and you can move on or pull over if another vehicle comes along.
- Without constant grading, even the slightest uphill will eventually develop a washboard of corrugated bumps. You're most likely to encounter them on the inside of uphill curves, but they can crop up almost anywhere. Hit these with any speed at all, and they can bounce you right off the road—not to mention rattling your car and your teeth.

- Approach blind curves with caution. Some forest roads are single lanes with turnouts for passing. On a curve, keep to your side of the road and take it slow. You could meet an oncoming vehicle— and it may be a big logging truck taking up the entire road.
- Use extra caution at stream fords. Getting to some of the trailheads in this book requires that you ford a stream one or more times. Before crossing, take a good look at what you'll be driving through. Does your vehicle have enough clearance that the undercarriage won't drag in the water? Is one side of the ford shallower than the other? Are there any obstacles in the water? Once you start across, take it slow. If the stream is in flood, don't try to cross it. This *is* Georgia, but it's not the place to play Dukes of Hazzard. On the other side, be sure to pump your brakes a few times while you're rolling to dry them out.
- Avoid these roads altogether during inclement weather. Winter snows can turn a mountain road into a toboggan course, and day after day of heavy rains or freezing and thawing temperatures can turn a hard-packed surface into mush.
- Always fill your gas tank before heading out.

On the Trail

Safety on the trail is as much about using good common sense as it is about anything else. Basically it boils down to so many do's and don't's, plus things to look out for. Here's a short list.

- Do let someone know your plans for the day before you go.
- Don't hike alone.
- Do dress appropriately and pack the items listed on p. 12.
- Don't start a long hike late in the day.
- Do keep your shoes on while crossing a creek or river.
- Don't cross a waterway in flood.
- Do carry plenty of drinking water.
- Don't drink water straight from the creek.

Things To Look Out For

It's rare to see a bear, but if you do, stand your ground.

Bears. Bears seem to be the number one thing people are afraid of encountering on a hike. In reality, the chances of meeting a bear on the trail are slim. When you do, the bear usually high-tails it for the nearest laurel thicket. Should you meet up with an aggressive bear, stand your ground. These animals can run much faster than you and they can climb trees. Make yourself look and sound as big as possible—wave your arms, shout, bang on something loud. This usually is enough to scare a bear away.

Snakes. Snakes are the second most feared thing in the woods. The chances of seeing a snake are good if you spend enough time outside. In the north Georgia mountains there are two types of venomous snakes to be concerned about—copperheads and rattlers (timber, pigmy, and eastern diamondback). Here again, use common sense. If you see or hear a snake in the trail, stop, assess the situation, and wait for the snake to move on or choose an alternate path around it.

The most common venomous snake in the woods is the copperhead.

Stinging Insects. There's nothing worse than bumping into a nest of angry hornets or disturbing a colony of yellow jackets or ground wasps. Such an encounter can quickly turn a peaceful walk in the mountains into a complete panic, with people running pell-mell through the woods screaming and tearing their clothes off. Those stings can hurt like the dickens, and for anyone who is severely allergic, they can be deadly. If you have such an allergy, never hike without your epi-pen. And everyone should always be on the lookout; hornets like to build their gray, football-shaped nests over water, so be especially careful around creeks and streams.

Poison Ivy. Of all the plants in the mountains, this one seems to be the most prolific. It grows just about everywhere, but it loves moist woodlands and areas around moving water. Since many a waterfall in north Georgia is guarded by the stuff, it's a plant you'll want to learn to recognize. Basically it grows in two ways—as a vine that climbs trees, and as individual plants living in vast colonies on the ground. Wading into a patch or grabbing hold of a hairy vine poses no immediate

Poison ivy grows on the ground and on hairy vines up trees.

threat, but wait about 24 hours and if you're allergic (as many people are), you'll develop a rash of intensely itchy red blisters wherever the plant touched your skin. If you've had more exposure than that, be prepared to suffer. The rash can take weeks to dry up and go away, often progressing to an oozy mess before it's gone. Should you inadvertently make contact, wash thoroughly with cold water in the nearest stream and hope for the best.

Crossing Streams

Using trekking poles while crossing a stream adds stability.

When you approach a stream crossing, size it up. Is it small enough to hop across? Are there stepping-stones, and do they seem stable? How deep is the water? Can you move upstream or downstream to find a better place to cross?

If you can hop across or use stepping-stones, by all means do. And if you don't already use a walking stick, look around you for a temporary one. Having three points of contact with the streambed makes you many times more stable.

Beware of crossing on logs. Sometimes a log can make for a good bridge, but it can also roll with you or break halfway across. Finally, if the water is more than ankle deep and/or 10 feet or more across, and especially if the bottom looks slippery, unclip the waist strap on your pack (if you fall in you'll want to be able to ditch it in an instant so it won't drag you downstream), clasp your hiking partner(s) by the arms, form a circle, and everyone walk across together. You'll be surprised at how you can negotiate across strong current, over slick rocks, through deep water using this method.

Waterfalls

Every year people die at waterfalls, and some have died at waterfalls listed in this book. Here's what usually happens. They try to climb up the cliff or steep slope beside a waterfall to get a better view or take a picture or make an attempt to reach the top, and then they slip and fall. They try to peer over the edge at the top, and then they slip and fall. They try to climb the waterfall itself, and then they slip and fall. Everything near a waterfall—rocks, roots, fallen trees—is wet and slippery.

If you do any of these things, it's only a matter of time before you slip and fall, too. At best you'll twist an ankle or break an arm; at worst it could be fatal. Certainly your mistake will ruin what could have been a nice hike for you and everyone else. *Always exercise extreme caution and common sense around waterfalls.*

Not all waterfalls have signs nearby to remind you of danger.

Hunting Season

During the fall and on select dates during the spring, if you're hiking in the national forest there's a chance you'll run into game hunters. Most of the time, especially during small game season, this is not a problem. However, on opening day of rifle deer hunting season, around major holidays, and during special "quota hunts," it *can* be a big deal. On these days, in some places, it can seem that the woods are full of hunters—and you might not be comfortable with that. Regardless of whether you are or not, it's a good idea to wear bright colors in the woods during hunting seasons. For specific hunting dates, check the website at www.gohuntgeorgia.com or call one of the wildlife contacts in Appendix A. Hunting is not allowed in Georgia state parks, so they are a safe bet any time of the year.

How To Use this Book

Information for each hike is broken down into different categories.

- **Hike Name**
  The hike name is at the top left side of the opening spread. Often this is also the name of the trail you will hike on.
- **Hike Data**
  Below the hike name you'll find the hike data.
      Distance is always total distance—how far you will walk from the time you leave the trailhead until you return to the trailhead.
      Type refers to the hike's route configuration. You might walk a loop, an out-and-back where you go to a certain point and then retrace your steps, a lollipop, T- or Y-shape, or some other variation.
      Difficulty is a rough approximation of how hard or easy you might find the hike route. It takes into account such things as length, elevation change, trail footing, location, etc.
      Start Elevation is the elevation in feet at the trailhead. Use this in conjunction with the map's elevation profile. If it's a high number like 3,800 feet, you'll likely start out at a high point and walk downhill at the beginning of the hike. A low number means you'll probably start out walking uphill.
      Total Ascent is the cumulative elevation gain over the course of the hike. The higher the number, the more strenuous the hike.
      Land Manager refers to the public agency that oversees the trails you will be walking on. In this book the agencies listed are abbreviated as follows: National Park Service (NPS), United States Forest Service (USFS), Georgia State Parks (State Park), and Georgia Department of Natural Resources (GA DNR).
      Fee refers to whether or not you'll have to pay a use fee or parking fee. For example, $5 means per vehicle and $3 pp means per person.
- **Hike Description and General Information**
  Following the first photo and hike data is a general description of the

hike and/or interesting information related to the hike or its location. This section is not meant for directional purposes.

- **Directions to the Trailhead**
  Specific driving directions to the trailhead are given, usually from the closest town. GPS coordinates for the trailhead are also provided.

- **Trailhead Locator Map**
  Located adjacent to the trailhead directions, this gives you a clear idea of where the trailhead is and shows the route given in the text.

- **Hiking Directions**
  These are turn-by-turn directions for the hike route. Use of a GPS is not a requirement for hiking, but the exact mileage is given for each turn or entry in the directions. This lets you know how far you've come and how far you still have to go to get to your destination. Hiking distance information was determined with a GPS receiver unit. FS indicates Forest Service road.

- **Route Map**
  All maps are to scale and show the hiking route and side trails you'll encounter. The elevation profile at the bottom of the map provides a basic idea of how much up and down walking to expect. Keep in mind that a short hike of under a mile, climbing 40 feet, descending 70 feet, and then climbing 30 feet may *look* more difficult than an eight-mile hike that gains 300 feet, descends 500 feet, and then climbs 200 feet. This is because every profile uses a different scale, determined by the elevation numbers along the side of the profile relative to the distance numbers along the bottom.

Northeast Georgia

VIEW FROM PINNACLE KNOB

🥾 Three Forks Trail

Hike Distance	3.0 miles
Type of Hike	Out & Back
Difficulty	Moderate
Hiking Time	Half Day
Start Elevation	2,357 ft
Total Ascent	1,000 ft
Land Manager	USFS
Fee	None

A boulder marks the entrance to Three Forks Trail.

On the old maps, the Three Forks Trail begins high atop Rabun Bald and continues all the way down to Three Forks, a spot which marks the beginning of the West Fork of Chattooga River. Nowadays most folks who hike the Three Forks trail begin at John Teague Gap on Overflow Creek Road. From here it's pretty much a downhill walk to the river.

The name Three Forks refers to the place where three streams, Holcomb Creek, Overflow Creek, and Big Creek, all come together to form the West Fork of the Chattooga River. Located within the Chattooga's Wild and Scenic corridor, it is a beautiful spot. You'll find Three Forks Trail well marked for the first mile. After that, pay close attention to the directions. Soon you'll traverse a steep slope above a noisy mini-gorge, and finally the trail dumps you out on a small point between Holcomb Creek and Overflow Creek. Directly in front of you, Big Creek crashes over a 30-foot waterfall. There are more waterfalls nearby on Holcomb Creek. It's a great spot for lunch before the climb back up and out.

Getting to the Trailhead

From Clayton, take Warwoman Road 13.8 miles and turn left on Overflow Creek Road (FS 86). Continue 4.0 miles to the trailhead at John Teague Gap.

GPS Coordinates
N 34° 57.73' W 83° 13.72'

★=Start

FS 86

28

441

FS 7

Clayton

Warwoman Road

Sandy Ford Rd

Warwoman Dell

Hiking Directions

Begin Walk past the granite trail marker and down Three Forks Trail.

Mile 1.0 Turn left on the old woods road, continuing downhill.

Mile 1.2 Reach Holcomb Creek. There's a big rock slab here overlooking a 30-foot slot waterfall. This is the uppermost falls you'll see on this creek on this hike. Head upstream 25 paces, under the overhanging bluff and around the big boulder. Carefully ford the creek just above the small rapid, then angle right into the woods. You should find a well-used but unmarked path which parallels Holcomb Creek above its mini-gorge. Follow this path as it

angles slowly downhill. Eventually it turns and heads straight down the mountain.

Mile 1.5 Scramble down the steep slope to Overflow Creek at Three Forks. There is a high waterfall directly across the stream on Big Creek and more falls on Holcomb Creek. The small campsite marks the turnaround point. From here, head back the same way you hiked in.

Mile 3.0 Finish.

Big Creek Falls at Three Forks.

Three Forks Trail Map

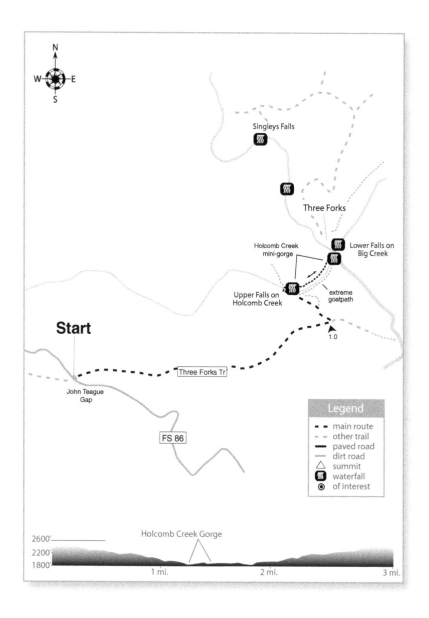

Singleys Falls

Three Forks

Holcomb Creek
mini-gorge

Lower Falls on
Big Creek

Upper Falls on
Holcomb Creek

extreme
goatpath

Start

1.0

Three Forks Tr

John Teague
Gap

FS 86

Legend

- - main route
- - - other trail
━━ paved road
── dirt road
△ summit
▧ waterfall
◉ of interest

Holcomb Creek Gorge

2600'
2200'
1800'

1 mi.   2 mi.   3 mi.

⚤ Holcomb Creek Trail

Hike Distance	1.9 miles
Type of Hike	Loop
Difficulty	Easier
Hiking Time	2 hours
Start Elevation	2,540 ft
Total Ascent	580 ft
Land Manager	USFS
Fee	None

Holcomb Creek Falls.

Northeast Georgia is known for spectacular waterfalls, and this short hike takes you past three of them—two on Holcomb Creek and another on Ammons Creek. Once at the trailhead you'll walk down a gently sloped foot trail to the various falls. A wooden bridge crossing Holcomb Creek serves as the viewing point for the taller, lower section of Holcomb Creek Falls, while a platform is provided at Ammons Creek Falls. You can view the upper falls on Holcomb Creek from low boulders across a small plungepool from the falls. This spot is also a great place to take a break and cool your feet. The final half mile of this loop hike is along FS 696. If you prefer to stick to the trails, just return the way you came in. Given that getting to the trailhead means a long drive on a bumpy dirt road, you might consider doing at least one more nearby hike while you are in the area. Starting points for both Three Forks (p. 24) and Rabun Bald (p. 30) are nearby.

Getting to the Trailhead

From Clayton, take Warwoman Road 10.1 miles, turn left on FS 7 (Hale Ridge Road), and drive a long, curvy, sometimes bumpy 6.6 miles to the trailhead at its intersection with FS 86. Park on the right, just before you get to the intersection.

GPS Coordinates

N 34° 58.69' W 83° 15.99'

★=Start

Hiking Directions

Begin Walk across FS 86. The small granite boulder with the trail name etched into the rock marks the beginning of Holcomb Creek Trail and the start of the hike.

Mile 0.3 Reach Holcomb Creek Falls. There is an observation platform/bridge across the creek here. After viewing the falls, continue along Holcomb Creek Trail.

Mile 0.5 Reach Ammons Creek Falls. There is an observation platform here as well. After viewing the falls, backtrack a

very short distance and turn right to continue on Holcomb Creek Trail. The turn onto this part of the trail may be hard to see. You'll soon begin to climb up and around Holcomb Creek Falls. You can hear it crashing over to your left.

Mile 1.1 The trail leads up past an upper sluice/slide waterfall 20 feet high on Holcomb Creek. After viewing the falls, continue on Holcomb Creek Trail.

Mile 1.3 Holcomb Creek Trail ends on FS 86 (Holcomb Creek Road). Turn left here and walk the road back to the trailhead.

Mile 1.9 Finish.

Holcomb Creek Trail Map

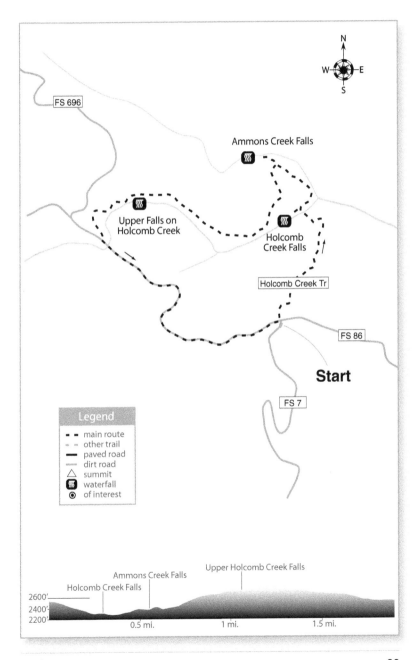

N
W E
S

FS 696

Ammons Creek Falls

Upper Falls on
Holcomb Creek

Holcomb
Creek Falls

Holcomb Creek Tr

FS 86

Start

FS 7

Legend
- - main route
- - other trail
— paved road
— dirt road
△ summit
🌊 waterfall
◉ of interest

Upper Holcomb Creek Falls

Ammons Creek Falls

Holcomb Creek Falls

2600'
2400'
2200'

0.5 mi.   1 mi.   1.5 mi.

⚡ Rabun Bald Trail

Hike Distance	6.0 miles
Type of Hike	Out & Back
Difficulty	Difficult
Hiking Time	Half Day
Start Elevation	2,545 ft
Total Ascent	2,154 ft
Land Manager	USFS
Fee	None

Hikers enjoy a 360-degree view from the top of Rabun Bald—the second highest peak in Georgia.

Although you don't really walk straight uphill for three miles to get to the top of Rabun Bald, it sometimes feels like it. No bones about it, this is a difficult hike. However, unless you have access to a helicopter, it's one of only two ways to get to the top of the second highest mountain in Georgia. The other way requires a much longer trek along the remote Bartram Trail.

All the difficulty aside, this is a fabulous hike. As you climb upwards of 2,000 feet in elevation, you'll pass through several different types of forests. Nearer the trailhead, look for the numerous tall white pine interspersed with oak and other species. These trees are indicative of a xeric oak-pine forest. Farther along, the trail tunnels through thick stands of mountain laurel bushes—what old-timers refer to as a "slick" or "hell." At the summit, which measures 4,696 feet above sea level, a stone tower stands above gnarled, windblown trees and shrubs. From the lookout platform, when the weather is clear, the views seem endless.

Getting to the Trailhead

From Clayton, take Warwoman Road 10.1 miles and turn left on Hale Ridge Road (FS 7). Continue 5.6 miles to the trailhead, an unmarked pulloff with room for just a few cars on the road shoulder. Look for the trail marker on the south side of the road where the trail heads steeply up the hill.

GPS Coordinates
N 34° 58.32′ W 83° 15.84′

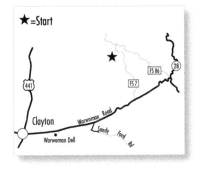

★=Start

Hiking Directions

Begin Walk up the wooden steps past the trail marker signs and up the mountain.

Mile 2.2 After much climbing, you'll come to a wide open area located on a saddle, sometimes used for camping. This is a good place to take a break. The trail gets very steep soon after this.

Mile 3.0 Reach the top of Rabun Bald. A stone lookout tower here has wooden steps leading to an observation platform. On the west side of the tower look for the trail junction with Bartram Trail. There's still a stone marker here with the old Three Forks Trail name emblazoned on its side. Return the way you came up.

Mile 6.0 Finish.

The Rabun Bald Trailhead, marked by a classic hiker sign.

Rabun Bald Trail Map

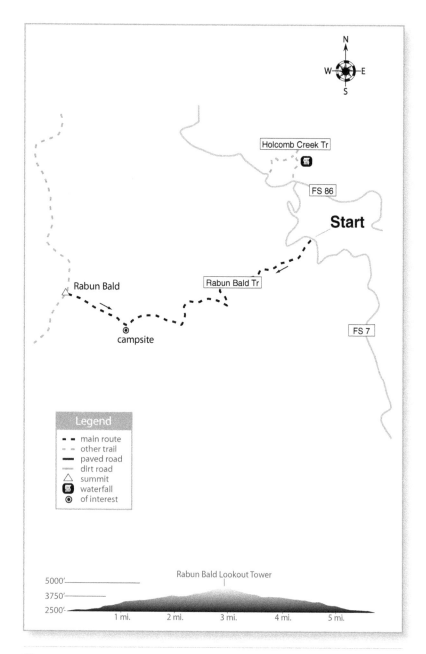

Holcomb Creek Tr

FS 86

Start

Rabun Bald

Rabun Bald Tr

campsite

FS 7

Legend
- **– –** main route
- – – other trail
- ▬▬ paved road
- ▬ dirt road
- △ summit
- 🌊 waterfall
- ◉ of interest

Rabun Bald Lookout Tower

5000'
3750'
2500'
1 mi. 2 mi. 3 mi. 4 mi. 5 mi.

𝄞 Pinnacle Knob View

Hike Distance	8.2 miles
Type of Hike	Out & Back
Difficulty	Moderate
Hiking Time	Half Day
Start Elevation	1,978 ft
Total Ascent	580 ft
Land Manager	USFS
Fee	None

From the top of Pinnacle Knob, you can see for miles.

There aren't many hikes where you can see beautiful waterfalls *and* get an amazing mountaintop view. The hike to Pinnacle Knob is one of those. From the quiet Warwoman Dell Recreation Area near Clayton, you'll hike along the Bartram Trail out past Becky Branch Falls and then Martins Creek Falls before heading up the mountain to the top of Pinnacle Knob. For the most part the trail is not too difficult, but once you turn onto the Pinnacle Knob Trail, the half mile to the top is pretty darned steep. Your reward is an awesome view from atop a high cliff. This is one of those clifftops that has plenty of more or less level rock surface along the top, great for sprawling out and resting your legs. Just be sure to stay away from the edge as it rounds down and then drops straight off into the abyss. Most of the view is to the north and east where you can spot other hiking destinations like Rabun Bald and Black Rock Mountain. Farther to the north are the high peaks of North Carolina.

Getting to the Trailhead

From Clayton, take Warwoman Road 2.9 miles to Warwoman Dell Recreation Area on the right. Drive to the trailhead parking at the end of the road in the picnic area.

GPS Coordinates

N 34° 52.89' W 83° 21.17'

★=Start

FS 86 28
441 FS 7
Clayton Warwoman Road
Sandy Ford Rd
★
Warwoman Dell
Recreation Area

Hiking Directions

Begin Walk back down along the road you drove in on, and turn left on the yellow diamond–blazed Bartram Trail. You'll go up and across Warwoman Road.

Mile 0.3 Cross on a footbridge just below 30-foot-high Becky Branch Falls. After viewing the falls, continue on the Bartram Trail as it winds around the ridge to the next watershed.

Mile 2.0 Pass the lower falls on Martins Creek, below and to your right. It's a 12-foot tiered drop followed by a pothole-filled sluice.

Mile 2.2 Reach Martins Creek Falls. There are two observation decks here. The upper deck looks

out on the high waterfall, while the lower deck looks down into a sluice forming the lower section of the falls. Walk off the back of the lower observation deck to continue on the Bartram Trail.

Mile 3.6 Turn left on Pinnacle Knob Trail. It's marked here as Trail #58.

Mile 4.1 Reach the clifftop view on Pinnacle Knob. Just beyond the view the trail ventures into the woods to the summit. If you look closely, you can locate the U.S. Geological Survey benchmark. (You can read about benchmarks on p. 181.) After enjoying the scenery, return the way you came.

Mile 8.2 Finish.

Pinnacle Knob View Trail Map

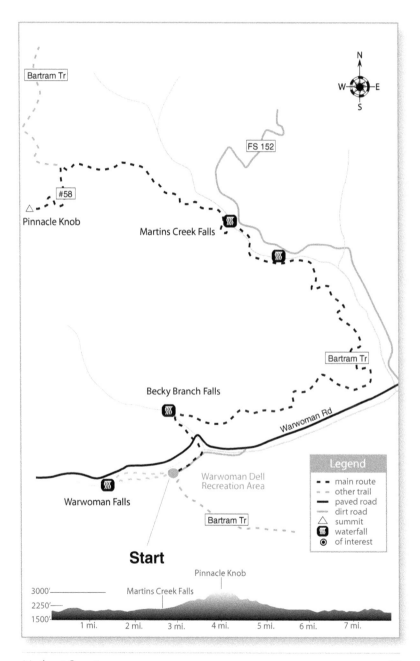

Bartram Tr

N
W–E
S

FS 152

#58

Pinnacle Knob

Martins Creek Falls

Bartram Tr

Becky Branch Falls

Warwoman Rd

Warwoman Dell
Recreation Area

Warwoman Falls

Bartram Tr

Start

Legend
- — — main route
- – – other trail
- —— paved road
- —— dirt road
- △ summit
- ▨ waterfall
- ◉ of interest

Pinnacle Knob

3000'
2250'
1500'

Martins Creek Falls

1 mi.   2 mi.   3 mi.   4 mi.   5 mi.   6 mi.   7 mi.

🥾 Tennessee Rock Trail

Hike Distance:	2.4 miles
Type of Hike	Loop
Difficulty	Easier
Hiking Time	2 hours
Start Elevation	3,270 ft
Total Ascent	587 ft
Land Manager	State Park
Fee	$5

A stone sign beside the trail marks the summit of Black Rock Mountain.

*B*efore you start this hike, be sure to stop in at the Park visitor center and pick up a copy of *An Interpretive Guide to the Tennessee Rock Trail.* Once on the trail you'll notice the numbered markers; there are 25 of them. For each marker there's a description in the guide that gives information pertaining to location. You'll learn about everything from wildflowers to different types of forests to weather patterns—and much more.

Tennessee Rock Trail makes a wonderful hike. For the most part it circles around the top of Black Rock Mountain, with one short but steep section that crosses its summit. However, the true highlight of the hike is walking up and over Tennessee Rock, which comes toward the end. Here you'll find an observation deck that overlooks Germany Valley to the west and the crest of the Appalachians. You can visually trace the route of the Appalachian Trail as it heads north through the Tray Mountain Wilderness and into North Carolina.

Getting to the Trailhead

From Clayton, drive north on US 441 to Mountain City and turn onto Black Rock Mountain Parkway. Drive up the mountain and at the T-intersection, turn right toward the visitor center. The trailhead is just up the road on the right.

GPS Coordinates
N 34° 54.44' W 83° 24.72'

Hiking Directions

Begin Walk past the picnic tables and onto the trail, going left to start the Tennessee Rock Trail. It's marked with yellow blazes. Soon the trail splits. Take the right fork up the wooden steps and turn right at the top to start the loop.

Mile 0.6 A side trail turns off to the left here, making a short spur over to interpretive sign #7.

Mile 1.3 Turn left off the old roadbed to stay on the route. Soon you'll begin a short but steep climb toward the summit.

Mile 1.7 Reach the summit of Black Rock Mountain. It's hard to miss the sign.

Mile 1.9 Walk up and over rocks to the Tennessee Rock overlook. Look west to view Germany Valley. A break in the trees on the opposite side of the trail looks east toward Rabun Bald and the Georgia/South Carolina border.

Mile 2.0 The trail bumps into the paved state park road, then banks back to the left into the woods without crossing. You'll see a sign here marking the Eastern Continental Divide.

Mile 2.3 Complete the loop and turn right, down the hill.

Mile 2.4 Finish.

Looking west from Tennessee Rock toward the Appalachian Trail.

Tennessee Rock Trail Map

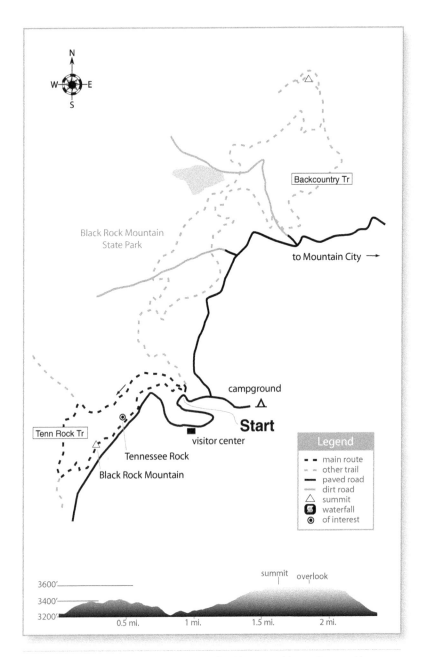

DAY HIKING THE NORTH GEORGIA MOUNTAINS

🚶 J.E. Edmonds Trail

Hike Distance	7.2 miles
Type of Hike	Loop
Difficulty	Moderate
Hiking Time	Half Day
Start Elevation	3,270 ft
Total Ascent	2,000 ft
Land Manager	State Park
Fee	$5

From Lookoff Mountain you can see the community of Rabun Gap.

The J.E. Edmonds Trail is the backcountry loop at Black Rock Mountain State Park. Typically state park backcountry trails are meant to be used by overnight backpackers. This one has four designated backcountry campsites for use by reservation only. However, it makes a great day hike as well.

The loop begins at the same point as the Tennessee Rock Trail but quickly heads off in the opposite direction. Most of the first mile is spent walking down the mountain (you'll have to walk back up at the end) before bottoming out and then working your way up and over two good climbs to get to the top of Lookoff Mountain. As the name implies, you can "look off" it from atop a high cliff. A cable fence discourages you from going over the edge—an unfortunate necessity to protect the foolhardy among us. From the overlook, loop up to the Lookoff Mountain campsite so you can claim the summit, continue on down near Black Rock Lake, and make your climb to the finish.

Getting to the Trailhead

From Clayton, drive north on US 441 to Mountain City and turn onto Black Rock Mountain Parkway. Drive up the mountain, and at the T-intersection turn right toward the visitor center. The trailhead is just up the road on the right.

GPS Coordinates
N 34° 54.44' W 83° 24.72'

★=Start

Black Rock Mountain State Park ★

US 441

Dillard

Mountain City

US 76

Clayton

Hiking Directions

Begin Walk past the picnic tables and onto the trail. You'll go right to start on J.E. Edmonds Trail. It's marked with orange blazes.

Mile 0.7 Turn right onto the east fork of J.E. Edmonds Trail.

Mile 0.8 Pass Fern Cove (campsite #1).

Mile 1.4 Cross a paved road after descending a steep hill.

Mile 2.3 Cross a bridge over a creek, then cross a road.

Mile 3.2 Bear left as an old road comes in from the right.

Mile 3.4 The East Fork section ends here. Continue straight out toward Lookoff Mountain. You'll soon return to this spot.

Mile 3.6 Turn right off the old roadbed to loop out to Lookoff Mountain Overlook.

Mile 3.8 Lookoff Mountain Overlook is down to your right. After taking in the view come back to this spot then continue up and over the mountain, passing campsite #2.

Mile 4.1 You should now be back at Mile 3.4. Bear right down the hill onto the west fork of the trail.

Mile 5.1 Cross a gravel road.

Mile 5.6 Pass a small waterfall and then a turnoff on your right that leads to the Creek Ridge (campsite #4).

Mile 6.0 Cross a gravel road.

Mile 6.4 Close the loop. Turn right and hike up the mountain the way you came down.

Mile 7.2 Finish.

J.E. Edmonds Trail Map

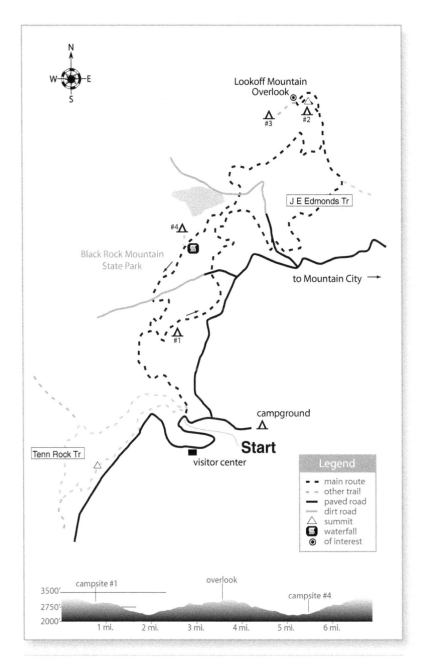

N
W—E
S

Lookoff Mountain
Overlook

△
#3

△
#2

J E Edmonds Tr

#4△

Black Rock Mountain
State Park

to Mountain City →

△
#1

campground
△

Tenn Rock Tr

△

Start

visitor center

Legend
- - main route
- - other trail
— paved road
dirt road
△ summit
waterfall
of interest

campsite #1

overlook

campsite #4

3500'
2750'
2000'
1 mi.   2 mi.   3 mi.   4 mi.   5 mi.   6 mi.

🥾 Whiteoak Stomp View

Hike Distance	5.3 miles
Type of Hike	Out & Back
Difficulty	Moderate
Hiking Time:	3 hours
Start Elevation	2,672 ft
Total Ascent	1,860 ft
Land Manager	USFS
Fee	None

The view from the outcrop at Whiteoak Stomp looks east toward Lake Burton.

You'll follow the Appalachian Trail for the entirety of this hike. Starting at Dicks Creek Gap on US 76 between Hiawassee and Clayton, the route takes you south, climbing up to high ridges and eventually ending at a clifftop view above the headwall of Whiteoak Stomp.

Whiteoak Stomp—what a name. Look on a topographical map of the Southern Appalachians, and you'll come across various areas called stomps. What the heck is a "stomp?" Is that what you're supposed to do along the AT—stomp on down the trail? That's probably not it. Are you stumped? Think about who used to live around here and how they lived. Most folks had animals that needed a place to graze. Often the cattle or horses would be driven into the high country during the warmer months for fresh pasture and as a respite from the heat. Places where the livestock tended to congregate were called stamps or stomps. Usually these spots were somewhat level and had a water source somewhere nearby.

Getting to the Trailhead

From US 441 in Clayton, drive west on US 76 for 16 miles to Dicks Creek Gap. Or, from the junction of GA 17/75 and US 76, drive east on US 76 for 7.8 miles to the gap. There are picnic tables here where the Appalachian Trail crosses the highway.

GPS Coordinates
N 34° 54.72' W 83° 37.13'

★=Start

Hiking Directions

Begin Walk across US 76 and head south onto the Appalachian Trail, following the white blazes.

Mile 1.0 A blue-blazed trail turns left, here leading to a pipe spring water source.

Mile 2.5 A wooden sign reading "vista" points to the left here. Take this trail out to the overlook.

Mile 2.6 Reach the rock outcrop overlook above Whiteoak Stomp.

After taking in the view, turn around and return via the AT the way you came.

Mile 5.3 Finish.

Pipe Springs

A pipe spring just off the Appalachian Trail.

Every so often while walking on a trail you'll come across a spring. More often than not, there will be a small piece of pipe jutting out, making it easier to fill a water bottle. Is this water safe to drink? The safe answer is: on the trail, always boil, treat, or filter water before drinking. But look at it this way—for hundreds of years, springs were the sole source for mountain family water consumption. For thousands of north Georgia folks today, they still are. You've heard the term "bottled at the source?" *This* is the source.

Whiteoak Stomp View Trail Map

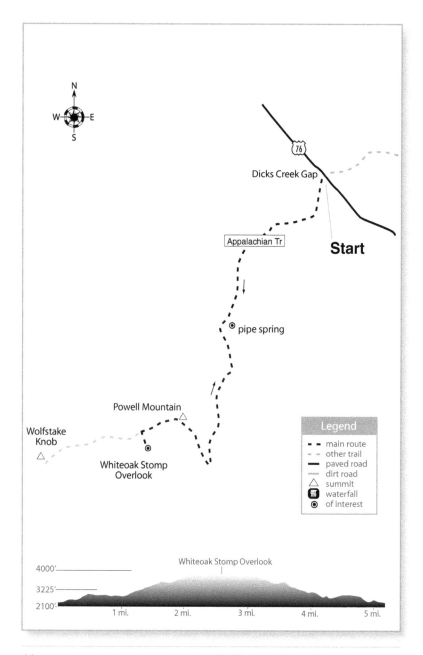

N
W E
S

76

Dicks Creek Gap

Appalachian Tr

Start

⊙ pipe spring

Powell Mountain
△

Wolfstake
Knob
△

Whiteoak Stomp
Overlook

Legend
- - - main route
- - - other trail
▬▬ paved road
▬ dirt road
△ summit
♨ waterfall
⊙ of interest

Whiteoak Stomp Overlook

4000'
3225'
2100'
    1 mi.   2 mi.   3 mi.   4 mi.   5 mi.

👣 Hemlock Falls Trail

Hike Distance	3.4 miles
Type of Hike	Out & Back
Difficulty	Easier
Hiking Time	Half Day
Start Elevation	2,025 ft
Total Ascent	615 ft
Land Manager	USFS
Fee	None

Hemlock Falls drops 15 feet into a nice plungepool.

You'll get your feet wet if you decide you want to see all the waterfalls on Moccasin Creek. Hemlock Falls Trail takes you past several waterfalls before seeming to come to an end at Hemlock Falls itself. Most folks turn back here for a shorter 2.2-mile hike. Look closely and you'll see the that a well-used but unmarked trail continues on. This is the route more adventurous day hikers take, and it requires fording Moccasin Creek above Hemlock Falls.

There are several ways to go about fording a stream on foot. Many people prefer to take off their shoes and socks and tiptoe through the water. This can work, but it makes for unstable going. Sooner or later you're going to slip on a slick rock, and then not only your shoes but everything else you're wearing will get wet as well. The best bet is to grab a hiking stick and forge across with your shoes or boots on. Your footing will be more secure, your boots will be no wetter than if you were hiking in the rain, and you'll be a quarter mile up the trail before the tiptoers get their shoes back on.

Getting to the Trailhead

From Clayton, take US 76 west for 11.0 miles and turn left on GA 197. Go 3.7 miles to Moccasin Creek State Park and the state fish hatchery. Turn right at the sign for Hemlock Falls. It's 0.5 mile to the trailhead.

GPS Coordinates
N 34° 50.87' W 83° 35.82'

★=Start

Hiking Directions

Begin Walk out beyond the stone trail sign and up along Moccasin Creek.

Mile 0.4 Pass a small feeder stream falls which you can see on the far side of Moccasin Creek.

Mile 0.5 Reach the first falls on Moccasin Creek, an 8-foot-high sluice. Continue on the trail.

Mile 0.6 Reach the second falls on Moccasin Creek, a 10-foot-high sluice. Continue on the trail.

Mile 0.7 Cross the creek on a narrow footbridge right over the top of a small waterfall.

Mile 0.8 Reach the third falls on

Moccasin Creek, a 12-foot-high drop followed by a 10-foot-high, 30-foot-long slide. Continue on the trail.

Mile 1.1 Reach Hemlock Falls, a 15-foot horsetail fan landing in a magnificent pool. Continue on up the right side of the falls. Up to this point you've been following a well-defined trail. As you ascend beyond Hemlock Falls, the trail becomes fainter and less well maintained. *Pay close attention here.* From the top of Hemlock Falls, step off 60 or so paces, then ford to the other side of Moccasin Creek, where the trail continues as you climb high above the creek.

Mile 1.7 Reach the fifth and up-permost falls on Moccasin Creek, the sixth waterfall of the hike. This is the best of the bunch, with a 40-foot triple tier on the left and a horsetail on the right, both landing in a nice pool. When you're ready, return the way you came.

Mile 3.4 Finish.

Hemlock Falls Trail Map

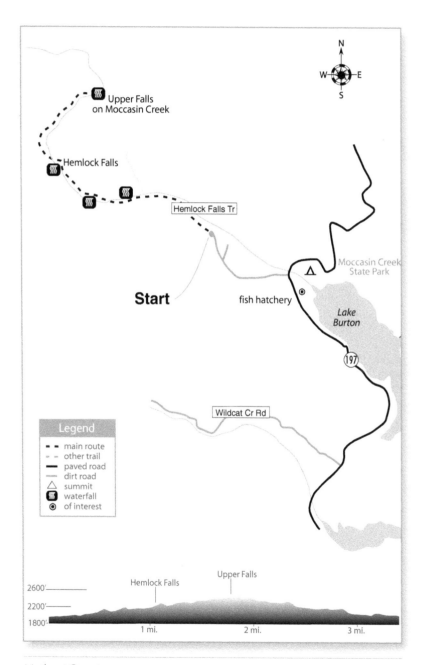

♦ Tallulah Gorge Circuit

Hike Distance	3.6 miles
Type of Hike	Loop
Difficulty	Moderate
Hiking Time	Half Day
Start Elevation	1,556 ft
Total Ascent	1,002 ft
Land Manager	State Park
Fee	$5

A high suspension bridge crosses the Tallulah River above Hurricane Falls.

Tourists flock to Tallulah Gorge, and it's no wonder. Here, the Tallulah River has scoured out a 600-foot-deep chasm containing five major waterfalls, while other smaller ones cascade over the cliffs from either side. Since the early 19th century, people have gawked at these wonders from above, sightseeing and enjoying the cool mountain breezes. Now that the Gorge is a state park, people still come to look, but they also come for adventure.

A hike down into Tallulah Gorge is an excellent adventure and not for the casual walker. Getting to the floor requires negotiating 500 steps (both down and back up), crossing a dizzying suspension bridge, fording the river, and then scrambling along the rocky shore next to several of the waterfalls.

Hiking in the gorge requires a permit. You can get one if you're one of the first 100 visitors the day you want to go, so arrive early. You'll also receive a map and safety instruction from a ranger. The gorge floor is closed on wet weather days due to slick rocks.

Getting to the Trailhead

Jane Hurt Yarn Interpretive Center at Tallulah Gorge State Park, just off US 441, south of Clayton.

GPS Coordinates
N 34° 44.41' W 83° 23.42'

★=Start

Clayton

76

441

Rabun Beach Campgrounds

Lake Rabun

Tallulah Gorge State Park

Hiking Directions

Begin From the interpretive center, go left on North Rim Trail. Remember your permit!

Mile 0.2 Reach overlook #1. Here you'll look down on Oceana Falls. Return the way you came, passing the interpretive center.

Mile 0.5 Reach overlook #3. View Hawthorne Pool. Turn left onto Hurricane Falls Trail.

Mile 0.5+ Reach overlook #2. View Tempesta Falls. The steps to the bottom start here. You'll descend them and cross the footbridge above Hurricane Falls, then turn left down the steps to the gorge floor.

Mile 0.7 Reach the gorge floor and Hurricane Falls viewing plat-

form. Ford the river here and turn right to rock-scramble downstream.

Mile 1.0 Reach Oceana Falls area. Cross underneath Caledonia Cascade, then work your way down the slab far to the left of Oceana, using friction to keep you on the rock.

Mile 1.4 Reach Bridal Veil Falls. There is a large pool here where swimming is allowed. It's a good thing, since you might get wet anyway if you slip while working your way down the rock by the falls. Return to the footbridge the way you came.

Mile 2.2 Back at Hurricane Falls, cross the river and climb steps up to the south rim.

Mile 2.5 Reach the top of the steps. Whew! Turn left to overlook #8.

Mile 2.6 Reach overlook #9 and then overlook #10. Retrace your steps to Hurricane Falls Trail, then continue straight on the South Rim Trail.

Mile 2.8 Reach overlook #7.

Mile 2.9 Reach overlook #6.

Mile 3.0 Cross bridge and turn right on North Rim Trail.

Mile 3.2 Reach overlook #5.

Mile 3.3 Reach overlook #4.

Mile 3.5 Reach overlook #3. Return from here to the interpretive center.

Mile 3.6 Finish.

Tallulah Gorge Circuit Trail Map

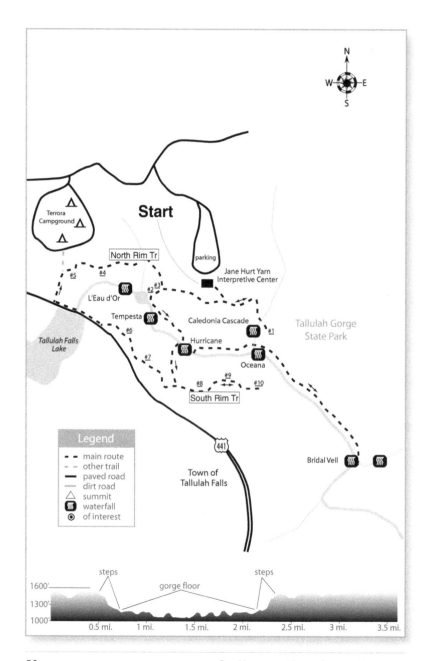

Legend
- - - main route
- - - other trail
— paved road
—— dirt road
△ summit
🌊 waterfall
⊙ of interest

　　　DAY HIKING THE NORTH GEORGIA MOUNTAINS

✹ Panther Creek Trail

Hike Distance	7.8 miles
Type of Hike	Out & Back
Difficulty	Strenuous
Hiking Time	Full Day
Start Elevation	1,509 ft
Total Ascent	1,147 ft
Land Manager	USFS
Fee	$3

The hike culminates at 75-foot-high Panther Creek Falls.

Based on the number of cars you're likely to see at the trailhead parking lot, you'll know this is a popular hike. Why shouldn't it be? The trailhead is easy to get to, and the destination is spectacular. Once on the trail, however, you'll be surprised at how few folks you encounter. This is usually the case with a longer trail. The reason is that people tend to hike at a consistent speed, and unless you start at the same time as those going the same way, you tend to encounter only others heading in the opposite direction, and they come and go quickly.

Several things make this a strenuous hike. The nearly eight-mile length is nothing to sneeze at, and there are a few steep grades to contend with. Mostly, though, it is the character of the trail that ratchets the difficulty up a notch. You are hiking in a wooded river gorge. In places the path literally clings to the hillside. Lean one way and you'll bump your head on the cliff rising above you, lean too much the other way and chances of a tragic fall increase dramatically. Needless to say, you must watch your step.

Getting to the Trailhead

From Tallulah Gorge State Park, drive south on US 441 for 2.6 miles and turn right on Old 441 South. Continue 1.5 miles to the trailhead.

GPS Coordinates
N 34° 41.92' W 83° 25.19'

★ =Start

Clayton

76

441

Tallulah Gorge State Park

Tallulah Falls

441

★

Old

Hiking Directions

Begin Walk across the road and onto Panther Creek Trail where you'll soon pass underneath the 4-lane.

Mile 0.9 Pass beneath an overhanging cave-like rock. Just beyond, you'll hear the crashing noise of the first waterfall down in the stream to your right.

Mile 2.6 Reach a bluff overlooking the second waterfall, a 15-foot waterslide.

Mile 3.7 After hiking along several stretches of trail where the path barely clings to the mountainside above the creek, you'll come to a high bluff overlooking Panther Creek Falls. It's a long way to the bottom. Up here you can view the top falls, a 35-foot tiered drop ending in a sluice. Follow the trail to the bottom.

Mile 3.9 Reach the bottom of Panther Creek Falls. This is a seriously big waterfall with a huge plungepool. It's a great place to take a swim or eat lunch. From here, return the way you came.

Mile 7.8 Finish.

A misstep here could send you tumbling down the mountain.

Panther Creek Trail Map

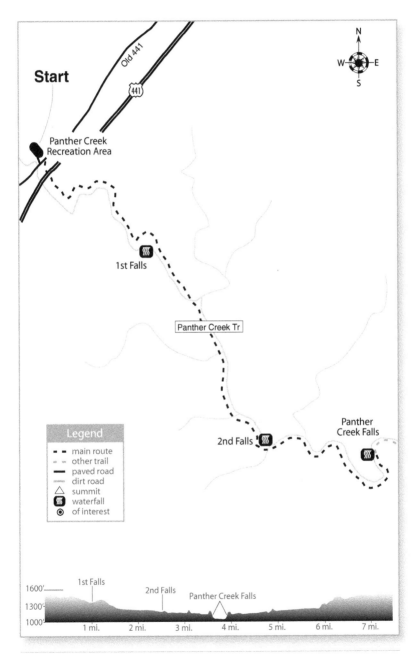

Start

Old 441

441

Panther Creek
Recreation Area

1st Falls

Panther Creek Tr

Panther
Creek Falls

2nd Falls

N
W—E
S

Legend
- - main route
- - other trail
— paved road
— dirt road
△ summit
▨ waterfall
◉ of interest

1600' 1st Falls
1300'   2nd Falls   Panther Creek Falls
1000'
        1 mi.   2 mi.   3 mi.   4 mi.   5 mi.   6 mi.   7 mi.

Chenocetah Mountain

Hike Distance	5.4 miles
Type of Hike	Loop
Difficulty	Moderate
Hiking Time	Half Day
Start Elevation	1,777 ft
Total Ascent	853 ft
Land Manager	USFS
Fee	None

Chenocetah Mountain's stone tower serves as the starting point of your hike.

Save this hike for a fall, winter, or spring outing. In summer it can be downright steamy, and the route tends to get a bit overgrown. Better yet, plan a day in mid-May to take advantage of the rhododendron bloom. Chenocetah Mountain claims to have one of the largest stands of *Rhododendron minus* (commonly known as Carolina Rhododendron) in the country. You'll hike past plenty of rhododendron bushes as the trail tunnels its way through them on your descent to Lake Russell, and you'll pass a small waterfall as well.

Once down in the Lake Russell Recreation Area, you'll walk beside the lake, through the picnic area, past the swimming beach, and finally past the campground before heading back up the mountain, returning to the stone fire tower that was your starting point. Built in the 1930s from native granite, it's the only stone firetower in Georgia. What does *Chenocetah* mean? It's a native American word signifying to "look all around." That sure fits.

Getting to the Trailhead

From GA 105 in downtown Cornelia, take Wyly road heading out of town. Go 0.7 miles and turn right on Chenocetah Drive. Go 1.2 miles and park at the tower.

GPS Coordinates

N 34° 30.07' W 83° 30.42'

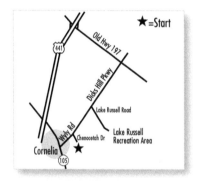

Hiking Directions

Begin Walk right up to the stone tower and continue past it on the old dirt road heading down the hill.

Mile 0.3 Turn right onto Rhododendron Trail. It's sporadically marked with green and sometimes blue blazes.

Mile 0.7 At the trails junction, bear left to remain on Rhododendron Trail.

Mile 1.5 Pass a small cascade down the hill on your right.

Mile 2.0 Turn right on the paved Lake Russell Road (FS 59).

Mile 2.3 Bear right at the information station, heading toward the beach and campground.

Mile 2.7 Turn left onto Lake Russell Trail, which parallels the road while following closer to the lake.

Mile 3.0 Arrive at the picnic area. Turn right up the steps and back onto the road, where you'll go left toward the swim beach and campground.

Mile 3.3 Pass campground Loop A on your left.

Mile 3.4 Turn right on Campground Trail, an old grass-covered road, and follow the green and sometimes blue blazes.

Mile 4.7 Complete the loop. Turn left to head up the mountain the way you came down.

Mile 5.4 Finish.

The trail follows the shoreline of Lake Russell.

Chenocetah Mountain Trail Map

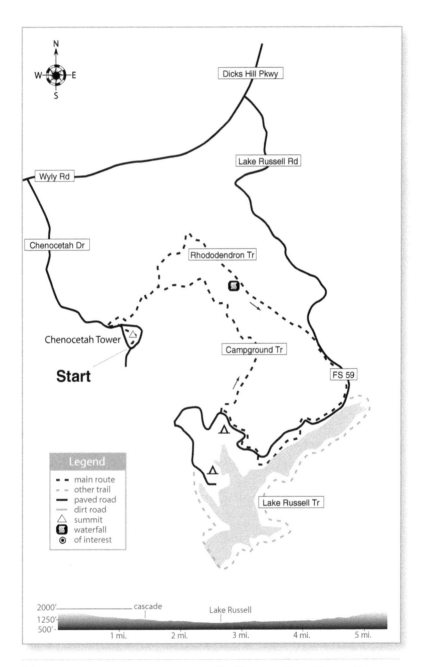

N
W—E
S

Dicks Hill Pkwy

Lake Russell Rd

Wyly Rd

Chenocetah Dr

Rhododendron Tr

Chenocetah Tower

Start

Campground Tr

FS 59

Legend

- - main route
- - other trail
— paved road
— dirt road
△ summit
▨ waterfall
◉ of interest

Lake Russell Tr

2000'
1250'
500'

cascade

Lake Russell

1 mi. 2 mi. 3 mi. 4 mi. 5 mi.

🥾 Nancytown Falls

Hike Distance	3.9 miles
Type of Hike	Loop
Difficulty	Easier
Hiking Time	Half Day
Start Elevation	1,066 ft
Total Ascent	541 ft
Land Manager	USFS
Fee	None

This lower falls on Nancytown Creek is a favorite spot to cool off on a hot day.

You'll find the hike to Nancytown Falls on Sourwood Trail in the Lake Russell Recreation Area a delightful stroll—and a good one when the higher mountains to the north are locked in a winter freeze. Lake Russell is in the mountains before the mountains. That is, they may feel like mountains to a lowlander, but compared to the higher peaks of the Blue Ridge, they are mere foothills. Still, once you're on the trail and hiking along, you'll enjoy the gentle grades.

Sections of this trail traverse stands of new-growth pine. These are areas that were logged not too many years ago, and pine is one of the first trees to grow back. Another is sourwood, for which the trail is named. Its tiny, bell-like, mid-summer blooms are the source of sourwood honey, a famous regional delicacy. Once out of the old cuts, the forest is more mature. Notice the difference; the trail holds together better here, and the air feels different—cooler on a warm day. This is a forest of mixed hardwoods. Nearer the creek, you'll find Carolina rhododendron in abundance.

Getting to the Trailhead

From US 441 Bus. in Cornelia, take Dicks Hill Parkway north 2.0 miles and turn right on Lake Russell Road. Drive another 1.9 miles down the hill, then turn left to follow the signs for the group camping area. Park at the gate.

GPS Coordinates
N 34° 29.95' W 83° 29.07'

Hiking Directions

Begin Walk around the gate and down the road toward the group camping area.

Mile 0.4 Just before the bridge, turn left on Sourwood Trail (#155).

Mile 1.3 Cross Nancytown Road. In another half-mile or so you'll cross over a ridge and begin to hear the falls up ahead.

Mile 1.8 Turn left on the spur trail to Nancytown Falls.

Mile 1.9 Reach Nancytown Falls, a 25-foot-high broken horsetail fan surrounded by mountain laurel and Carolina rhododendron. After viewing the falls, retrace your steps on the spur trail, then continue on around the loop.

Mile 2.2 Pass through the remnants of an old beaver pond, now filled in. The trail follows Nancytown Creek, passing several small shoals and falls.

Mile 2.9 Turn right on FS 92. Immediately on your right are the lower falls on Nancytown Creek, a 10-foot, double-tiered drop with a shallow plungepool at the bottom.

Mile 3.3 Turn left on FS 591.

Mile 3.5 Go around the gate, over the bridge, and bear left on the paved road. This completes the loop. To return to the trailhead, continue on the paved road.

Mile 3.9 Finish.

Nancytown Falls Trail Map

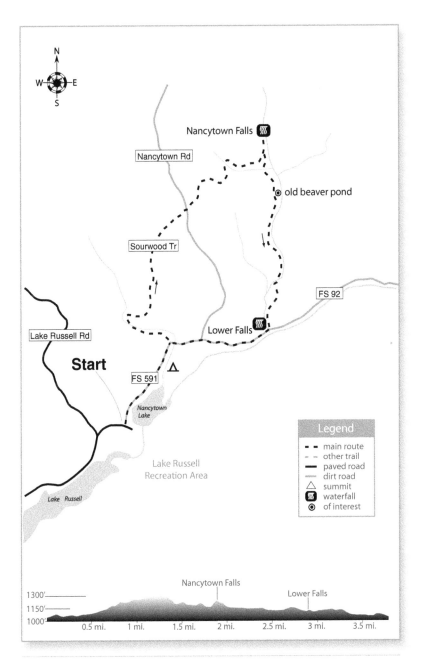

Legend
- - main route
- - other trail
— paved road
— dirt road
△ summit
▨ waterfall
◉ of interest

Eastern Blue Ridge

SUNRISE FROM BRASSTOWN BALD

![hikers icon] Miller Trek

Hike Distance	6.5 miles
Type of Hike	Loop
Difficulty	Moderate
Hiking Time	Half Day
Start Elevation	1,958 ft
Total Ascent	1,530 ft
Land Manager	USFS
Fee	None

The elaborate entrance to Miller Trek.

With all the fanfare at the grand entrance of this loop trail, you'd think the sights you see along the route would be nothing short of remarkable. Yes, it's a nice hike, and when the leaves are off the trees in late fall, winter, and early spring, there are some pretty good views. Perhaps its most salient attraction is a good show of wildflowers in spring. Beyond that, it's simply a nice walk in the woods—no waterfalls, no clifftop views, no lookout towers.

Miller Trek is named for former governor Zell Miller of Georgia and his wife, Shirley. According to the marker at the beginning of the loop, they loved this valley and wanted to set aside a natural area for future generations to enjoy. With the creation of this trail, that goal has been accomplished.

Be aware that Miller Trek begins and ends on the Brasstown Valley Resort property. You'll see the resort's informational signs and cross its trails early on in the hike. There's a special "hiker's parking lot" just down the road from the trailhead.

Getting to the Trailhead

Follow US 76/GA 515 north from Young Harris and turn right into the Brasstown Valley Resort on Brasstown Valley Road. You'll see a directional sign for Miller Trek at the turn off the highway. Park in the hiker's trailhead parking lot.

GPS Coordinates

N 34° 57.03' W 83° 50.52'

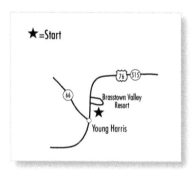

★=Start

Hiking Directions

Begin Walk from the trailhead parking lot out onto the main road and up past the tennis courts and golf course. You'll see the entrance to the Miller Trek at the far end of the employee parking lot on your right. The trail is initially blazed orange, but changes to green blazes once on USFS property.

Mile 0.6 Turn right at lower end of loop trail.

Mile 0.7 Turn right and cross under powerline.

Mile 1.2 Turn right to stay on the Miller Trek. If you were to go

left, you could do a much shorter lower 2.5-mile loop.

Mile 3.9 Cross long footbridge over a small stream drainage.

Mile 4.8 Continue straight to stay on Miller Trek. The trail entering from the left is the cutoff trail for the shorter loop.

Mile 5.4 Cross under the powerline and turn left to stay on Miller Trek.

Mile 5.6 Reach a 5-way junction of trails. Follow the trail straight ahead with the sign indicating the way to the trailhead.

Mile 5.7 Complete the loop. Bear right toward the trailhead and head back the way you came in.

Mile 6.5 Finish.

A long footbridge crosses a small creek drainage.

Miller Trek Trail Map

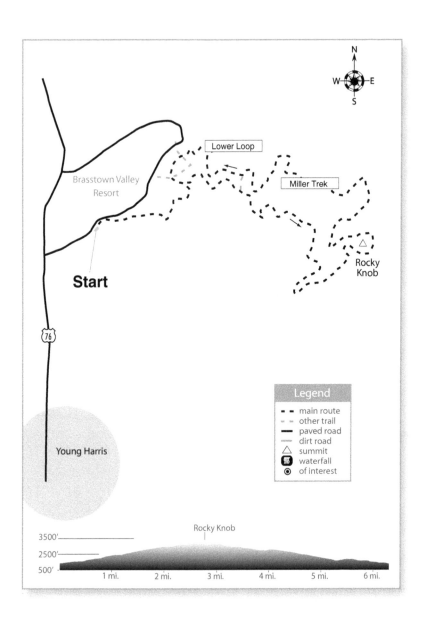

Lower Loop

Miller Trek

Brasstown Valley
Resort

Rocky
Knob

Start

76

Young Harris

Legend

- - main route
- - other trail
— paved road
— dirt road
△ summit
🌊 waterfall
◉ of interest

Rocky Knob

3500'
2500'
500'

1 mi.   2 mi.   3 mi.   4 mi.   5 mi.   6 mi.

🥾 Arkaquah Trail

Hike Distance	12 miles
Type of Hike	Out & Back
Difficulty	Strenuous
Hiking Time	All Day
Start Elevation	2,255 ft
Total Ascent	3,712 ft
Land Manager	USFS
Fee	None

The tower atop Brasstown Bald is still a long way off from this vantage point.

There are a number of ways to walk to the top of Brasstown Bald, Georgia's highest peak, and this is by far the most challenging. It also has the biggest payoffs—bragging rights and a number of spectacular views from rock outcrops.

You'll start the hike at the Track Rock Archaeological Site, where ancient petroglyphs are chiseled into a large boulder. Take a look at them before you start, because you'll likely be too tired afterward. Be prepared for difficult hiking. The steep first 1.5 miles takes you quickly to Locust Log Ridge, a knife-like spine with clifftop views. You'll cross over Chimneytop Mountain and then a saddle connecting to Brasstown Bald, from whence you'll hike the paved trail to the summit. In your hiking attire you'll stand out from the tourists who've arrived at the top by car, so be ready for lots of questions. Go ahead and brag a bit about your arduous trek to the top while you visually trace your route and rest up for the return trip. Should you choose to do this hike one-way with a shuttle, remember—it's easier on the knees to hike up than it is to hike down.

Getting to the Trailhead

Begin at the Track Rock Archaeological Site. Follow GA 180 from the bottom of Brasstown Bald for 4.8 miles. Turn right at the Track Rock sign onto Town Creek School Road and go 2.2 miles. Turn right on Track Rock Church Road and go 3.1 miles. Turn right on Track Rock Road and go 0.8 miles to the trailhead parking area.

GPS Coordinates

N 34° 52.92' W 83° 52.69'

Hiking Directions

Begin Walk across the road and onto the Arkaquah Trail.

Mile 1.7 You should now be hiking along a knife-like spine. The tower atop Brasstown Bald can be seen a long way off.

Mile 4.2 Summit of Chimneytop Mountain. Elevation 4,303 feet.

Mile 5.5 Reach the Brasstown Bald parking lot. There are picnic tables and a small store here as well. Bear right onto the paved summit trail.

Mile 6.0 Reach the summit of Brasstown Bald, Georgia's highest peak at 4,784 feet. There is a tower here as well as a visitor center and museum. After taking in the sights, return the way you hiked up.

Mile 12.0 Finish.

One of many view spots on the long ridge leading to Brasstown Bald.

Arkaquah Trail Map

Start

Track Rock Rd

Track Rock

view

view

Arkaquah Tr

view

views

Chimneytop
Mountain

Brasstown
Bald

Wagon TrainTr

parking lot

Jacks Knob Tr

N
W · E
S

Legend

- - - main route
- - - other trail
— paved road
— dirt road
△ summit
☷ waterfall
◉ of interest

summit tower

4700'
3500'
2000'

1 mi. 2 mi. 3 mi. 4 mi. 5 mi. 6 mi. 7 mi. 8 mi. 9 mi. 10 mi. 11 mi.

Brasstown Bald Summit

Hike Distance	1.2 miles
Type of Hike	Out & Back
Difficulty	Easier
Hiking Time	2 hours
Start Elevation	4,399 ft
Total Ascent	385 ft
Land Manager	USFS
Fee	$3

Amazing views await you from the lookouts atop Brasstown Bald.

If the Arkaquah Trail is the most difficult route to the summit of Brasstown Bald, the Summit Trail is by far the easiest. This is a hike most anyone can do. First of all, before making the climb up, you drive most of the way to the top and park in what has to be the largest trailhead parking lot in the state. No wonder the trail is paved: A single day of this parking lot's worth of people would wear out a natural-surface trail. Expect to see a lot of people on this popular hike.

The trail itself is not difficult, even though you'll gain close to 400 feet. It's wide enough for walkers to pass and has numerous benches along the way should you need to stop and catch your breath.

Once at the top, you're in for a treat. First of all, the views are truly spectacular, just as you would expect at the state's highest point. Also, the visitor center has an interpretive museum with all sorts of information—everything from early forestry practices to the natural history of the mountain itself.

Getting to the Trailhead

From Helen, take GA 17/75 north up the mountain through Unicoi Gap. Descend the mountain and turn left on GA 180. Continue 5 miles to GA 180 Spur where you'll turn left and travel 3 miles to the top parking lot.

GPS Coordinates
N 34° 52.19′ W 83° 48.63′

Hiking Directions

Begin Walk to the end of the parking lot and bear left at the gift shop onto the paved Summit Trail. Just beyond you'll pass the turnoff to the Wagon Train Trail.

Mile 0.6 Reach the summit, the visitor center, and lookout tower. Give yourself plenty of time here to take in the views and enjoy the visitor center. You can't go any higher in Georgia, so turn around here and go down the way you came up.

Mile 1.2 Finish.

At 4,784 feet, Brasstown Bald is Georgia's highest mountain.

Brasstown Bald Summit Trail Map

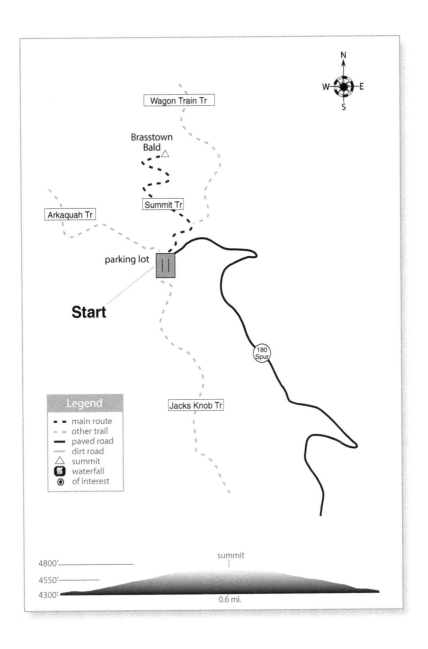

Wagon Train Tr

Brasstown Bald △

Summit Tr

Arkaquah Tr

parking lot

Start

180 Spur

Jacks Knob Tr

Legend
- - main route
- - other trail
— paved road
— dirt road
△ summit
▨ waterfall
◉ of interest

4800'
4550'
4300'

summit

0.6 mi.

Wagon Train Tr

Brasstown
Bald △

Summit Tr

Arkaquah Tr

parking lot

Start

180
Spur

Legend

- ■ ■ main route
- – – other trail
- ▬ paved road
- — dirt road
- △ summit
- 🌊 waterfall
- ◉ of interest

Jacks Knob Tr

summit

4800'
4550'
4300'

0.6 mi.

🚶 Wagon Train Trail

Hike Distance	2.6 miles
Type of Hike	Out & Back
Difficulty	Easier
Hiking Time	2 hours
Start Elevation	4,399 ft
Total Ascent	336 ft
Land Manager	USFS
Fee	$3

Hiking out on Wagon Train Trail leads you into the Brasstown Wilderness.

Can you imagine travelling up to the top of Brasstown Bald by wagon? Based on what you see on this trail, it would have been a long, bumpy ride—and quite a day's outing to travel all the way from Young Harris.

On this hike, you'll start near the summit of Brasstown Bald and walk out to the first good view along Wagon Train Trail. It's a great way to escape the hordes who hike to the summit and also your chance to venture into the Brasstown Wilderness. If you can walk around the mall, you can do this hike. At no point does it feel as if you are walking uphill, even though at times you are. The path is relatively wide—it's an old road and the footing is pretty good in most places, although there can be muddy spots to negotiate. The view at the far end is well worth the trip. You'll be looking to the northwest, out toward Young Harris and the valley where US 76 winds. Enjoy the walk.

Getting to the Trailhead

From Helen take GA 17/75 up the mountain north through Unicoi Gap. Descend the mountain and turn left on GA 180. Continue 5.0 miles to GA 180 Spur where you'll turn left and travel 3.0 miles to the top parking lot.

GPS Coordinates
N 34° 52.19' W 83° 48.63

Hiking Directions

Begin Walk to the end of the parking lot and bear left at the gift shop, onto the paved Summit Trail.

Mile 0.1 Turn right onto Wagon Train Trail. Soon you'll pass the Wilderness boundary sign.

Mile 1.3 After walking alongside a cliff formed from dynamite blasting when the original road was built, you'll come to an opening along the top of a cliff and an incredible view. Retrace your steps from here.

Mile 2.6 Finish.

You'll get a great view looking northwest from Wagon Train Trail.

Wagon Train Trail Map

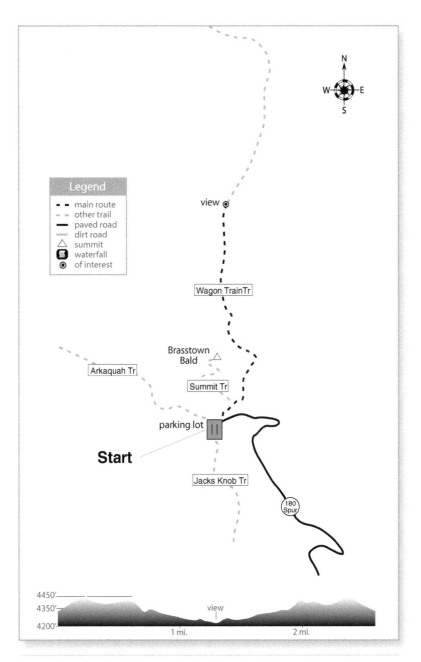

Legend
- - main route
- - other trail
— paved road
--- dirt road
△ summit
▓ waterfall
◉ of interest

view ◉

Wagon TrainTr

Brasstown Bald △

Arkaquah Tr

Summit Tr

parking lot

Start

Jacks Knob Tr

180 Spur

4450'
4350'
4200'
view
1 mi.   2 mi.

🥾 Wolfpen Ridge

Hike Distance	5.8 miles
Type of Hike	Out & Back
Difficulty	Moderate
Hiking Time	Half Day
Start Elevation	2,937 ft
Total Ascent	1,813 ft
Land Manager	USFS
Fee	None

You'll find this view as you near the parking lot atop Brasstown Bald.

Certainly you could just drive to the top of Brasstown Bald from the same place you start this hike, but this guide is for hikers, not drivers. One benefit of hiking is that, though you expend a lot of energy hiking up the steep mountainside, you don't have to spend the $3 it costs to park at the top.

The hike starts at Jacks Gap, where GA 180 Spur turns off GA 180. It's not really the bottom of Brasstown Bald, but from a hikers standpoint, you'll be hiking up the entire mountain.

The climb begins right away. The intensity varies, but for the most part you'll be climbing until you reach the summit. The grade is not so difficult, and there are only a few steep pitches to contend with on the way to Wolfpen Ridge, the on-ramp for the summit push. Once at the summit parking lot, you'll switch trails and take the paved Summit Trail to the very top. Don't expect to see many people on Jacks Knob Trail, but expect to see lots and lots of people on Summit Trail.

Getting to the Trailhead

From Helen take GA 17/75 up the mountain north through Unicoi Gap. Descend the mountain and turn left on GA 180. Continue 5 miles to GA 180 Spur. Park where Jacks Knob Trail crosses the highway.

GPS Coordinates
N 34° 50.87' W 83° 47.93'

Hiking Directions

Begin Walk up from the parking pulloff and onto Jacks Knob Trail. The trail climbs steadily up to Wolf-pen Ridge, then ascends with level sections along the way.

Mile 1.9 A small gap in the trees on the right side of the trail offers a good view to the southeast.

Mile 2.2 Reach the summit parking lot. Cross to the far side and take Summit Trail, which starts just to the left of the gift shop.

Mile 2.9 Summit of Brasstown Bald, with a lookout tower, observation deck, and visitor/interpretive center. After taking in

the sights, retrace your steps to the parking lot to end the hike.

Mile 5.8 Finish.

Carsonite markers like this one are commonly seen along the trail.

Wolfpen Ridge Trail Map

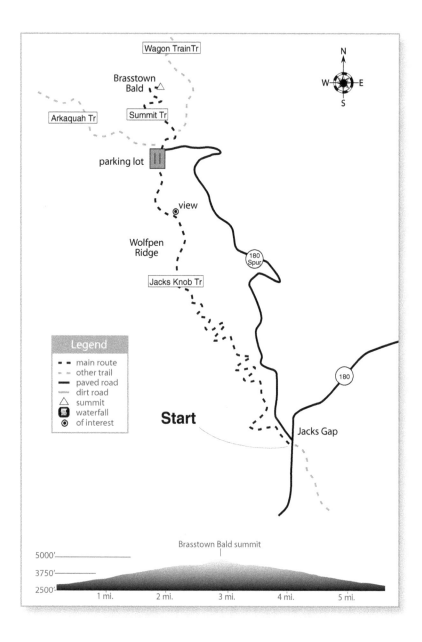

Wagon Train Tr

Brasstown Bald △

Arkaquah Tr

Summit Tr

parking lot

⊙ view

Wolfpen Ridge

180 Spur

Jacks Knob Tr

Start

180

Jacks Gap

N
W ✳ E
S

Legend
- ▪ ▪ main route
- ▪ ▪ other trail
- ▬ paved road
- ▭ dirt road
- △ summit
- ▦ waterfall
- ⊙ of interest

Brasstown Bald summit

5000'
3750'
2500'

1 mi.   2 mi.   3 mi.   4 mi.   5 mi.

🥾 Chattahoochee Source

Hike Distance:	4.7 miles
Type of Hike	Out & Back
Difficulty	Moderate
Hiking Time	Half Day
Start Elevation	2,937 ft
Total Ascent	1,645 ft
Land Manager	USFS
Fee	None

The mighty Chattahoochee River starts here at this small mountain spring.

All rivers must start somewhere, and the Chattahoochee begins at a strong spring high in north Georgia's eastern Blue Ridge. Two shallow, sink-sized pools are formed before the stream snakes through serpentine rock and heads downhill toward Atlanta and the Gulf. You can hike right to this spring; it's a water source for backpackers tramping along the Appalachian Trail (read more about mountain springs on p. 43).

You'll begin your hike at Jacks Gap, where Jacks Knob Trail crosses GA 180 and GA 180 Spur turns up the mountain to Brasstown Bald. The trail rises quickly from the highway and soon enters the Mark Trail Wilderness. Your destination is the Appalachian Trail at Chattahoochee Gap, climbing steeply as you stairstep up the mountains, leveling off or descending, then climbing again to get there.

Once at the gap, look for the trail sign pointing to water. This trail will lead you down the other side of the gap to the spring known as the source of the Chattahoochee River. Be sure to take a good long drink. This is the cleanest and purest the Chattahoochee will ever be.

Getting to the Trailhead

From Helen, take GA 17/75 up the mountain north through Unicoi Gap. Descend the mountain and turn left on GA 180. Continue 5.0 miles to GA 180 Spur. Park here where Jacks Knob Trail crosses the road.

GPS Coordinates
N 34° 50.87' W 83° 47.93'

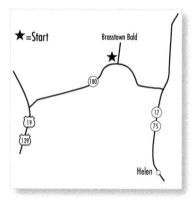

Eastern Continental Divide

The Eastern Continental Divide is the high point of land that determines which rivers flow into the Atlantic Ocean and which ones flow into the Gulf of Mexico. In north Georgia, the streams flowing to the Atlantic generally flow south either into the Savannah River system or the Chattahoochee River system. Those flowing generally north head into the Tennessee River system. This hike takes you over the Eastern Continental Divide when you cross the Appalachian Trail.

Hiking Directions

Begin Walk across the highway and up Jacks Gap Trail heading south.

Mile 2.2 Reach Chattahoochee Gap and Appalachian Trail. Follow the sign pointing down the other side of the gap toward water.

Mile 2.3 Reach the spring that's the source of the Chattahoochee River. After taking a drink and looking around, return via the gap the way you came.

Mile 4.7 Finish.

A sign at Chattahoochee Gap directs you to the water source.

Chattahoochee Source Trail Map

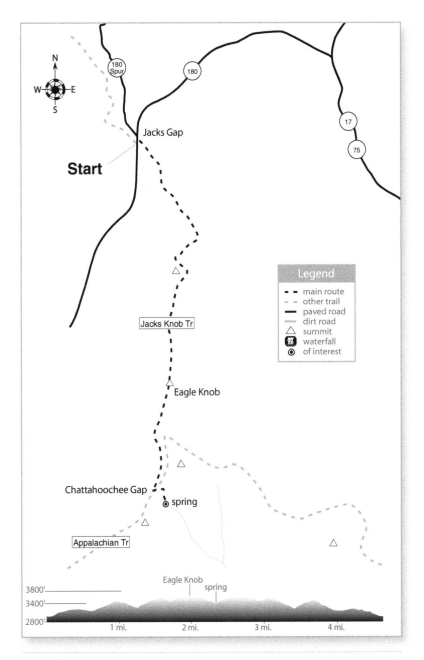

Legend
- - - main route
- - - other trail
— paved road
— dirt road
△ summit
♨ waterfall
◉ of interest

🥾 High Shoals Trail

Hike Distance	2.8 miles
Type of Hike	Out & Back
Difficulty	Easier
Hiking Time	Half Day
Start Elevation	2,873 ft
Total Ascent	950 ft
Land Manager	USFS
Fee	None

High Shoals Falls is the second of two waterfalls you'll see on this walk.

Hiking out to see a waterfall is high on many an outdoorsperson's list as a good way to spend a morning or afternoon. On this excursion you'll see two waterfalls, High Shoals Falls and Blue Hole Falls, both aptly named. High Shoals Falls is 125 feet, to be exact. The trail brings you right to the bottom of the waterfall, where you can look up into the mist as it comes crashing down a jagged cliff face. Just upstream is Blue Hole Falls, the first waterfall you'll get to on the hike. Here, the stream drops 30 feet into a deep blue pool. If the weather's hot, you might want to take a dip here—it's 20 feet deep and cold, cold, cold.

The trail to these falls is well marked and easy to navigate. Just follow the well-worn path blazed with green markers. Although you'll walk down to the waterfalls and then back up to your vehicle, it's a gentle grade in both directions. Most folks should be able to do this hike without too much difficulty.

Getting to the Trailhead

From Unicoi Gap on GA 17/75 north of Helen, drive north for 2.0 miles and turn right on FS 283. Ford the stream and continue another 1.3 miles to the trailhead, which is marked. *Caution:* Creek ford on FS 283.

GPS Coordinates
N 34° 48.97' W 83° 43.62'

★=Start

Hiking Directions

Begin Walk downhill on the green-blazed trail.

Mile 0.7 Cross the creek on a wooden bridge.

Mile 1.0 Look down to your left and you can see the top drop of Blue Hole Falls. Directly below it is a 25-foot drop into a big blue plungepool. Just beyond here a side trail leads to a viewing platform at the base of the falls. After a good look at this one, continue on down the trail.

Mile 1.2 The trail splits here. Take the left fork, which is still marked with green blazes.

Mile 1.4 Reach the viewing platform at the bottom of High Shoals Falls. What a waterfall! It drops 125 feet as it fans out over the rock cliff. Once you've had enough of it, return to the trailhead the way you came.

Mile 2.8 Finish.

Good signage and green blazes lead the way along High Shoals Trail.

High Shoals Trail Map

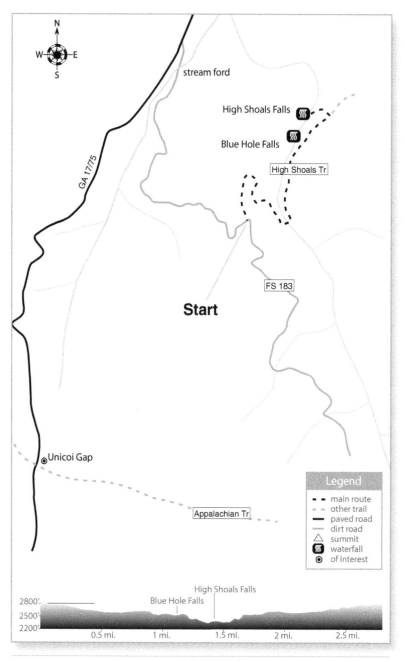

stream ford

High Shoals Falls

Blue Hole Falls

High Shoals Tr

GA 17/75

FS 183

Start

Unicoi Gap

Appalachian Tr

Legend

- - main route
- - other trail
— paved road
— dirt road
△ summit
▓ waterfall
◉ of interest

High Shoals Falls

Blue Hole Falls

2800'
2500'
2200'

0.5 mi. 1 mi. 1.5 mi. 2 mi. 2.5 mi.

🥾 Tray Mountain Summit

Hike Distance	5 miles
Type of Hike	Out & Back
Difficulty	Moderate
Hiking Time	Half Day
Start Elevation	3,113 ft
Total Ascent	1,469 ft
Land Manager	USFS
Fee	None

An Appalachian Trail thru-hiker pauses
atop Tray Mountain on his way to Maine.

Summiting a high mountain is always a thrill, especially when the top
is bare and there is a good view to be had. Tray Mountain is such a
one. Northbound Appalachian Trail thru-hikers encounter Tray Mountain
soon after entering the Tray Mountain Wilderness, usually toward the end
of their first week of hiking. Day hikers can tackle Tray Mountain, too, in
much less time.

Hikers arriving on the summit of Tray Mountain will find a razorback
outcrop of rock sticking up from the scrubby vegetation. It's a wonderful
vantage point with clear views in all directions. You can see Lake Burton
to the east, Brasstown Bald to the northwest, Mt. Yonah to the south,
and wave upon wave of blue ridges.

The hike itself begins at Indian Grave Gap after driving in on a
long dirt road. You'll walk along the AT, following the Tennessee Valley
Divide, to Tray Gap. Along the way you'll spot Tray Mountain through
breaks in the trees, lying like a sleeping dragon. Tray Gap marks the
start of a steep ascent to the summit.

Getting to the Trailhead

From Unicoi Gap on GA 17/75 north of Helen, drive north for 2.0 miles and turn right on FS 283. Ford the stream and continue another 3.7 miles to the trailhead at Indian Grave Gap. *Caution:* Creek ford on FS 283.

GPS Coordinates
N 34° 47.56' W 83° 42.86'

Hiking Directions

Begin Walk north on the Appalachian Trail.

Mile 0.7 Cross FS 79.

Mile 1.7 Reach Tray Gap. Cross FS 79 here again and begin ascent of Tray Mountain.

Mile 2.5 Reach summit of Tray Mountain. This is a good place to take a break and enjoy the views. Retrace your steps to Indian Grave Gap.

Mile 5.0 Finish.

★ =Start

The tower atop Brasstown Bald is just visible from the top of Tray Mountain.

Tray Mountain Summit Trail Map

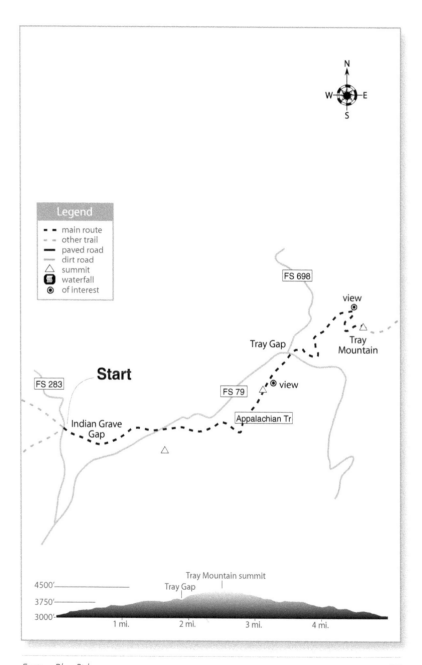

⛰ Rocky Mountain Loop

Hike Distance	7.2 miles
Type of Hike	Loop
Difficulty	Strenuous
Hiking Time	3/4 Day
Start Elevation	2,077 ft
Total Ascent	2,185 ft
Land Manager	USFS
Fee	None

From Rocky Mountain you'll look out over Helen to view Mt. Yonah to the south.

No matter how you do the Rocky Mountain Loop, you'll have to start out by hiking up a pretty steep incline. It is possible to begin at Unicoi Gap and follow the Appalachian Trail to get to the loop. On this route, you'll get there via the less-well-traveled Andrews Cove Trail to Indian Grave Gap, where the loop portion begins of the hike begins.

The Rocky Mountain Loop route is actually made up of two trails and a forest road. Once you get to Indian Grave Gap you'll begin it by walking down Indian Grave Gap Road. Strolling along the dirt road is a nice reprieve from the steep trail you just came up. After a little over half a mile you'll turn onto the Rocky Mountain Trail, which is not at all rocky. In fact, it gently climbs up to the AT which takes you up and over the top of Rocky Mountain. Up here you'll find an awesome rock outcrop with a view that looks directly toward Mt. Yonah, the mountain with the large cliff face, way off in the distance. Soon the trail dumps you back at Indian Grave Gap, where you drop down a steep two miles to the finish.

Getting to the Trailhead

From Helen, drive north on GA 17/75 towards Unicoi Gap. After about 5.0 miles turn left into the Andrews Cove Campground. The small trailhead parking lot is at the back of the campground next to sites #6 and #7.

GPS Coordinates
N 34° 46.76' W 83° 44.10'

★=Start

Hiking Directions

Begin Walk up the blue-blazed Andrews Cove Trail. The last half-mile before Indian Grave Gap is very steep.

Mile 1.9 Reach Indian Grave Gap. Bear left on Indian Grave Gap Road (FS 283).

Mile 2.5 Turn left on Rocky Mountain Trail, marked with blue blazes.

Mile 3.7 Reach the AT. Turn left up the mountain.

Mile 4.2 Here you come to a large rock outcrop with an amaz-ing view. This is a great place to take a break before continuing on.

Mile 4.3 Reach yet another good view spot.

Mile 5.3 Reach Indian Grave Gap to finish the loop. Turn right down Andrews Cove Trail to return to the trailhead.

Mile 7.2 Finish.

Rocky Mountain Trail tunnels along the flank of Rocky Mountain.

Rocky Mountain Loop Trail Map

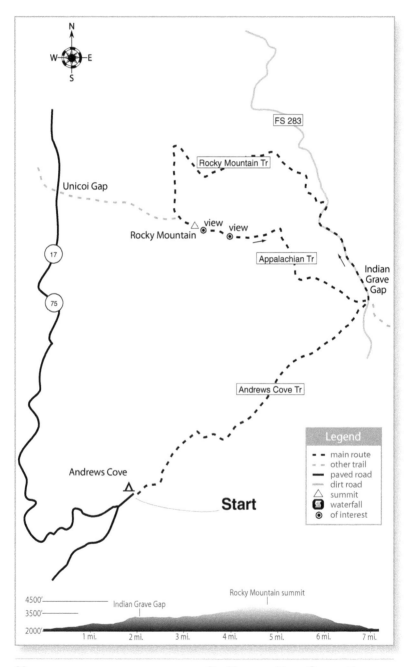

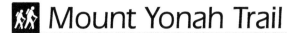

Mount Yonah Trail

It's not uncommon to see climbers and rap-
pellers on the rock faces of Mt. Yonah.

Hike Distance	4.8 miles
Type of Hike	Out & Back
Difficulty	Moderate
Hiking Time	Half Day
Start Elevation	1,740 ft
Total Ascent	1,623 ft
Land Manager	USFS
Fee	None

For decades, Mt. Yonah has been a magnet for rock climbers. One look at its high cliffs and you can see why. Outdoor groups from nearby colleges come here to learn rappelling, and frequently the Fifth Army Training Battalion from Camp Frank D. Merrill—the Army Rangers—come here to train for military operations. It's a great place to hike up and watch the action.

Be sure to look up toward the mountain before beginning this hike. High above you, hanging over the trailhead parking lot, are the cliffs and summit of Mt. Yonah. It's quite a sight, and you can see where you'll be once you reach the top. The trail itself meanders, with many shortcut trails to negotiate, before settling down to a designated path. Partway up you'll come to a nice group campground used by the Army Rangers. From here it's not too far to the cliffs, where the views are spectacular whether there are climbers or not.

Getting to the Trailhead

From the junction of GA 17 and 75 at the Indian Mound south of Helen, drive south on GA 75 for 3.3 miles and turn left on Tom Bell Road (CR 78). Go 0.2 miles and turn left again on Chambers Road (CR 79). From here go 0.7 miles and turn left on FS 323. It's 0.4 miles on this bumpy gravel road to the trailhead.

GPS Coordinates

N 34° 38.24' W 83° 43.52'

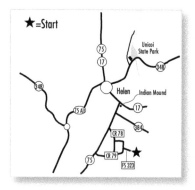

Hiking Directions

Begin Walk up Mt. Yonah Trail from the parking lot.

Mile 1.3 Reach a small clearing with a good view from a boulder outcrop. From here continue up the steep, washed-out road.

Mile 1.7 Turn right on FS 324.

Mile 1.8 Reach group camping area. There's an impressive row of toilets here. Bear right off the road and back onto the trail.

Mile 2.0 Reach the top of the cliff wall. Be careful not to venture too close to the edge. The trail continues along the edge of the cliff heading towards the mountain summit.

Mile 2.3 Reach a large field that crowns the summit of Mt. Yonah. You can bet helicopters transporting troops land here frequently. You can either continue across the field and loop around by way of the old roadbed that takes you down to the group campsite or return the way you came. In either case, from the campsite, retrace your steps to the trailhead.

Mile 4.8 Finish.

This sign is posted halfway up the mountain and not at the trailhead! Be sure to call ahead as it suggests, but call *before* you leave home.

Mount Yonah Trail Map

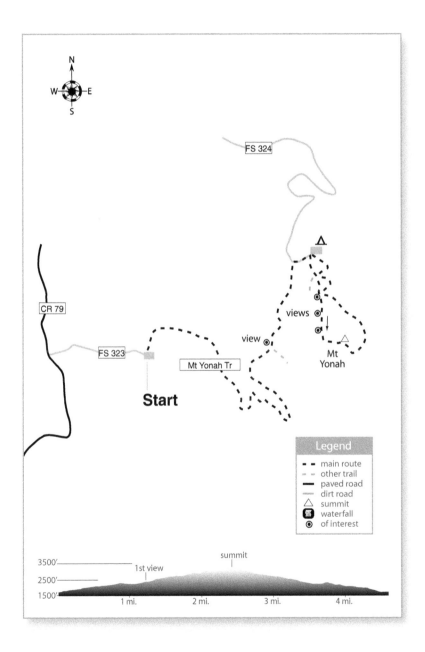

N
W—E
S

FS 324

△

CR 79

FS 323   Mt Yonah Tr

views ◉

view ◉   ◉ views

△
Mt
Yonah

Start

Legend
- - main route
- - other trail
— paved road
— dirt road
△ summit
🌊 waterfall
◉ of interest

3500'
2500'   1st view
1500'

summit

1 mi.   2 mi.   3 mi.   4 mi.

🥾 Dukes Creek Falls Trail

Hike Distance	2.2 miles
Type of Hike	Out & Back
Difficulty	Easier
Hiking Time	2 hours
Start Elevation	2,131 ft
Total Ascent	400 ft
Land Manager	USFS
Fee	$3

Two high waterfalls meet at the viewing platform for Dukes Creek Falls.

Some places in the Chattahoochee National Forest are so popular that in order to protect the resource, the Forest Service charges a fee—most times it's a parking fee. This way there's plenty of money to provide adequate parking, bathroom facilities, trail maintenance and construction, and observation platforms with railings so that folks don't tumble into a stream.

Dukes Creek is one of these places. At the trailhead, you'll find a nice parking lot, picnic tables, and vault toilets with a view. The trail to the falls is wide and easy to negotiate, descending so gradually you hardly feel it. The viewing platform puts you right in front of Dukes Creek Falls, a 250-foot-high waterfall that spreads out in all directions as it cascades over a wide cliff. Interestingly, the falls itself is on Davis Creek and it *falls* into Dukes Creek. Dukes Creek has its own waterfall; this tiered falls drops 35 feet, and the two waterfalls meet where Dukes Creek and Davis Creek converge. All together, it's an impressive sight and well worth the walk and the $3 fee.

Getting to the Trailhead

From Helen, take GA 75 Alt. for 2.2 miles. Turn right on GA 348, drive 2.0 miles and turn left up the entrance road to the Dukes Creek Falls trailhead parking area.

GPS Coordinates
N 34° 42.11' W 83° 47.34'

★=Start

Hiking Directions

Begin Follow the paved trail which starts just to the right of the toilets.

Mile 0.1 An observation deck provides a long-range view of Dukes Creek Falls for those who don't care to make the hike. Continue from here down a set of wooden steps.

Mile 0.3 Reach the bottom of the steps. A trail that begins near the Raven Cliffs trailhead parking area enters here. Make a hard turn back to the left to walk on a wide trail high above the creek.

You can hear and barely see several waterfalls crashing down below.

Mile 0.9 The trail narrows noticeably here as you continue your gradual descent.

Mile 1.1 Reach two wooden viewing platforms built to optimize the view of the falls. Dukes Creek Falls is right in front of you, crashing in all directions across a high cliff face. It's actually on Davis Creek. The other waterfall is on Dukes Creek proper and is also impressive. The bottoms of the two waterfalls meet, and the effect is stunning. When you've had enough of the falling water, return the way you came.

Mile 2.2 Finish.

Dukes Creek Falls Trail Map

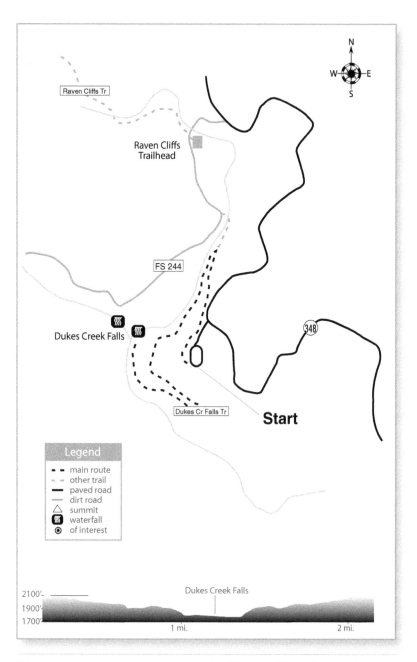

Raven Cliffs Tr

Raven Cliffs
Trailhead

FS 244

Dukes Creek Falls

348

Dukes Cr Falls Tr

Start

N
W E
S

Legend

- - main route
- - other trail
— paved road
— dirt road
△ summit
▧ waterfall
◉ of interest

Dukes Creek Falls

2100'
1900'
1700'
1 mi.
2 mi.

🥾 Raven Cliffs Trail

Hike Distance	6 miles
Type of Hike	Out & Back
Difficulty	Moderate
Hiking Time	Half Day
Start Elevation	2,028 ft
Total Ascent	1,200 ft
Land Manager	USFS
Fee	None

The waterfall at Raven Cliffs is one of the most dramatic in north Georgia.

This hike into the Raven Cliffs Wilderness takes you to one of north Georgia's most interesting sights—a high waterfall that drops down in a split in the cliff. The cliffs themselves are impressive enough, forming a bowl shaped headwall well over 100 feet high. Right in the middle is the waterfall, crashing down over a number of unseen drops before revealing itself through a crack in the rock face.

Hiking along the Raven Cliffs Trail is fairly easy. The trail follows the remains of an old logging railroad, so the grade is as gentle as it gets. You'll walk alongside Dodd Creek the entire way, and the real treat is this: three more waterfalls to enjoy as you go. You may want to extend this hike from a half day to a full day and really take your time. Several of the falls have pools deep enough to splash around in, and if it's too cool to get wet, you can take a lunch break on a sunny rock with a waterfall view. Once you get out to the cliffs, expect steep terrain around the base of the falls.

Getting to the Trailhead

From Helen, take GA 75 Alt. for 2.2 miles. Turn right on GA 348, drive 3.0 miles and turn left on FS 244 to the Raven Cliffs trailhead parking area.

GPS Coordinates

N 34° 42.57' W 83° 47.32'

★=Start

Hiking Directions

Begin Walk across FS 244 and onto Raven Cliffs Trail.

Mile 0.4 The first falls, a 15-footer, is on the left below the trail.

Mile 0.8 Pass a small, 8-foot broken sluice falls.

Mile 1.3 Second falls, a 15-foot plunge into a pool followed by a 15-foot slide.

Mile 1.6 You are now at a cliff area high above a 30-foot horsetail drop. You'll have to scramble off the trail to reach the base.

Mile 3.0 The trail reaches the absolute base of Raven Cliffs Falls and then heads steeply up the

hill beside it to a cleft in the cliff where the most dramatic part of the waterfall may be seen. The top is still a long way up, hidden between more rock clefts. You can see where people have scaled their way up trying to reach the top of the falls via a series of sketchy-looking, hand-over-hand, pull-yourself-up trails. Don't be tempted to try it. The view of the falls really does not get any better than from the base of the cleft. Enjoy it, then head back the way you came.

Mile 6.0 Finish.

The second waterfall on Dodd Creek.

Raven Cliffs Trail Map

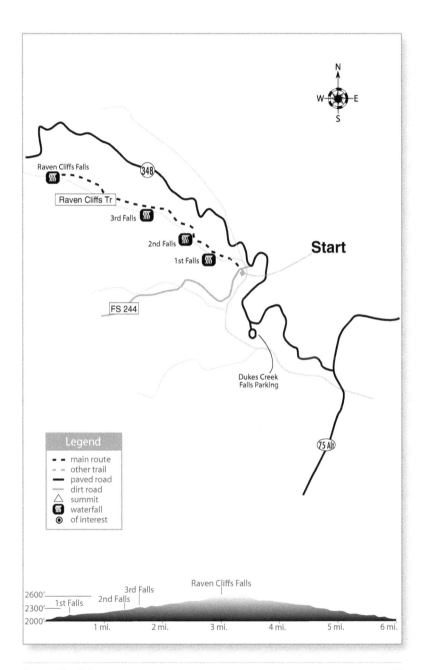

Raven Cliffs Falls

Raven Cliffs Tr

3rd Falls

2nd Falls

1st Falls

348

Start

FS 244

Dukes Creek
Falls Parking

75 Alt

N
W—E
S

Legend
- - - main route
- - - other trail
— paved road
— dirt road
△ summit
waterfall
⊙ of interest

2600'
2300'
2000'
1 mi.   2 mi.   3 mi.   4 mi.   5 mi.   6 mi.

1st Falls   2nd Falls   3rd Falls   Raven Cliffs Falls

☗ Whitley Gap Shelter

Hike Distance	3.3 miles
Type of Hike	Out & Back
Difficulty	Easier
Hiking Time	Half Day
Start Elevation	3,485 ft
Total Ascent	860 ft
Land Manager	USFS
Fee	None

Appalachian Trail hikers get breakfast
going at Whitley Gap Shelter.

On the Appalachian Trail you can hike the entire route from Georgia to Maine and spend every night with a roof over your head thanks to a system of shelters. Each one is unique: A-frame-style, log cabin, single story, double story, elaborate, or simple. Folks sleep on the floor or on raised platforms. Somewhere nearby is always a privy and a water source. Each one also has a journal where various hikers make daily entries, which make a fun read.

Whitley Gap shelter, like many AT shelters, is located off the trail, in this case a little over a mile down a side trail. There are good reasons for this. One of the primary reasons here is the proximity to a water source. Also, by locating the shelters off the main route, campers are allowed a sense of privacy—if such a thing exists in an eight-person shelter.

On this hike, you'll walk from Hogpen Gap up the AT to the top of Wildcat Mountain. A side trail leads out the ridge to the shelter. Along the way is a fantastic mountaintop view.

Getting to the Trailhead

From Helen, take GA 75 Alt. for 2.2 miles. Turn right on GA 348 and drive to Hogpen Gap where the AT crosses. Park on the east side of the road.

GPS Coordinates

N 34° 43.56' W 83° 50.39'

★ =Start

Hiking Directions

Begin Walk down the east side of the road 100 feet and then cross over on the AT, southbound. You'll immediately enter the Raven Cliffs Wilderness as you climb up from the gap.

Mile 0.3 Turn left at the top of the climb at the sign pointing to Whitley Gap Shelter on the Whitley Gap Trail.

Mile 0.5 First open rock outcrop view.

Mile 0.8 Second open rock outcrop view.

Mile 1.4 Reach Whitley Gap Shelter. There's room for about eight hikers to sleep here and space for several tents in the open woods out front. You might want to take a break here for lunch or a trail snack. Retrace your steps to the AT.

Mile 2.8 Reach the AT atop Wildcat Mountain. Turn left on the AT.

Mile 2.9 Here you'll find another view spot, this time from atop a cliff, which looks out over the Raven Cliffs Wilderness to the south. After soaking in the view, return to the trailhead via the AT the way you came up.

Mile 3.3 Finish.

The view from the rock outcrop atop Wildcat Mountain.

Whitley Gap Shelter Trail Map

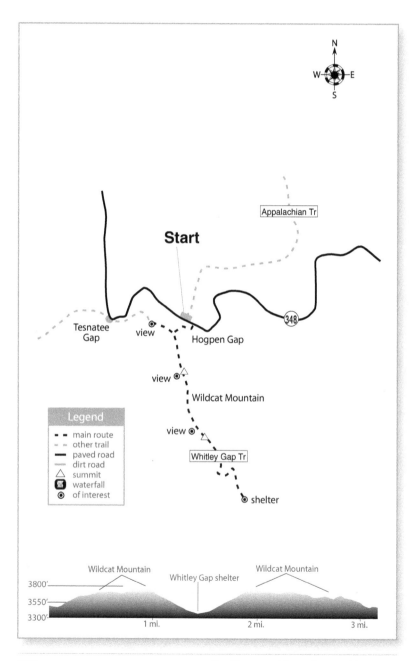

Appalachian Tr

Start

Tesnatee
Gap

view

Hogpen Gap

348

view

Wildcat Mountain

view

Legend
- - main route
- - other trail
— paved road
— dirt road
△ summit
▧ waterfall
◉ of interest

Whitley Gap Tr

◉ shelter

Wildcat Mountain
3800'
Whitley Gap shelter
Wildcat Mountain
3550'
3300'
1 mi.
2 mi.
3 mi.

 Cowrock Mountain View

Hike Distance	2 miles
Type of Hike	Out & Back
Difficulty	Easier
Hiking Time	2 Hours
Start Elevation	3,156 ft
Total Ascent	700 ft
Land Manager	USFS
Fee	None

White blazes mark the Appalachian Trail's route across Cowrock Mountain.

Want to take a short hike on the Appalachian Trail to an outstanding view? Drive up from Helen to Tesnatee Gap on the Richard Russell Scenic Highway, hop out of the car, and you can be at Cowrock in an hour or less.

It's amazing how in such a small amount of time you can get a feel for what it's like to hike along the legendary AT. This is America's most famous foot trail and it stretches all the way from Georgia to Maine. It's so well trodden that it seems impossible to lose your way. Even so, it's clearly marked with white blazes, whether on a tree, a rock, or a downtown sidewalk. Signs are posted at all trail or road intersections, and all trails leading to water are blazed blue.

On this hike you'll begin by walking gradually uphill and continue uphill all the way to the top of Cowrock Mountain, encountering numerous switchbacks along the way. The view from the rock is well worth the effort of this climb.

Getting to the Trailhead

From Helen, take GA 75 Alt. for 2.2 miles. Turn right on GA 348, drive to Hogpen Gap where the AT first crosses. From here, continue another 0.5 miles to Tesnatee Gap. The AT crosses through the gap but does not cross the road. Park in the pulloff on the west side of the road.

GPS Coordinates

N 34° 43.54' W 83° 50.84'

★=Start

Hiking Directions

Begin Walk south on the AT from the parking pulloff.

Mile 0.5 Reach a rock outcrop. There is a good view here looking back toward Wildcat Mountain.

Mile 1.0 Reach a large rock outcrop after numerous switchbacks. This is the top of Cowrock Mountain. It's a great place to sprawl out on the rock and take a well-deserved break. You'll retrace your steps from here.

Mile 2.0 Finish.

Spotting Wildflowers

At Cowrock, yellow ragwort blooms right off the trail.

On any hike you take in spring, summer, or fall, you are going to see at least some wildflowers in bloom—usually quite a few. For many folks, learning to spot and identify wildflowers is a central part of the hiking experience. One worthwhile item to carry in your daypack is a wildflower guidebook, preferably a small, portable one. It's nice to know what flower you're looking at. If your reference book is too big and heavy to take along, photograph the bloom, including the foliage if possible, then look it up when you get home.

Cowrock Mountain View Trail Map

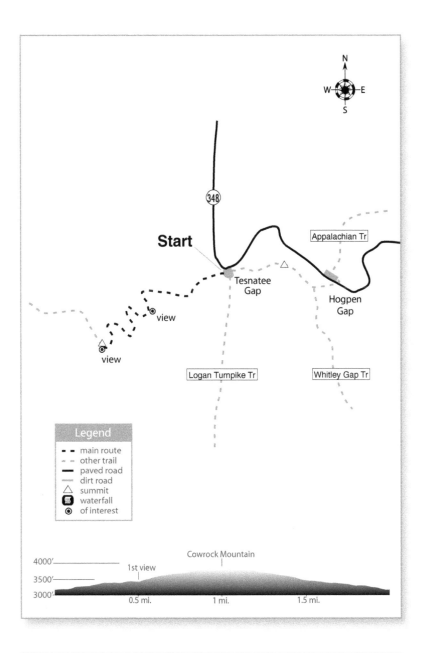

🥾 Bear Hair Gap Trail

Hike Distance	5 miles
Type of Hike	Loop
Difficulty	Moderate
Hiking Time	Half Day
Start Elevation	2,318 ft
Total Ascent	860 ft
Land Manager	State Park
Fee	$5

A highlight of the Bear Hair Gap Trail is the overlook view of Lake Trahlyta.

Of the two day hikes you can do at Vogel State Park, this is the shorter and less difficult one. You can of course go for a walk around Lake Trahlyta or on the nature trail, but neither of those is long enough to be considered a serious day hike.

Just the name Bear Hair Gap Trail brings up images of black bears waiting for you in the woods. As with any trail in the north Georgia mountains, you might see a bear on Bear Hair, but rest assured they are not lying in wait to attack you. Most folks consider themselves lucky to catch a glimpse of a bear, so do keep your eyes peeled for one.

The hike starts out along a trail section that is also the end of the Coosa Backcountry Trail. Soon you'll turn off it and head up and over a low knob which comes off a shoulder of Blood Mountain. Atop the knob a side trail leads out to a view through the trees of Lake Trahlyta far below. This is where you started, so it's interesting to see just how far you've come. To finish, it's a downhill walk back to the trailhead.

Getting to the Trailhead

The hike begins at Vogel State Park, located on US 19/129 south of Blairsville and north of Dahlonega. Park in the lake lot across from the visitor center and check-in station.

GPS Coordinates
N 34° 45.97′ W 83° 55.42′

Hiking Directions

Begin First check in at the visitor center to get a hiking permit. Then walk up past cabin #7 to the trailhead.

Mile 0.2 Turn right onto the combined Bear Hair Gap/Coosa Backcountry Trail.

Mile 0.6 Turn left here to start the loop. You're still on the combined Bear Hair Gap/Coosa Backcountry Trail.

Mile 2.1 Turn right here on the Bear Hair Gap Trail. The Coosa Backcountry Trail continues straight ahead.

Mile 2.8 Turn right on the spur trail to Lake Trahlyta overlook.

Mile 2.9 Reach the overlook. Continue around the small loop and return to Bear Hair Gap Trail.

Mile 3.1 Turn right back onto Bear Hair Gap Trail.

Mile 3.7 Turn right off the old roadbed and back onto foot trail.

Mile 4.3 Bear right to rejoin far end of Coosa Backcountry Loop.

Mile 4.4 Complete loop. Turn left to retrace your steps to the visitor center.

Mile 5.0 Finish.

Bear Hair Gap Trail winds through a section of large boulders.

Bear Hair Gap Trail Map

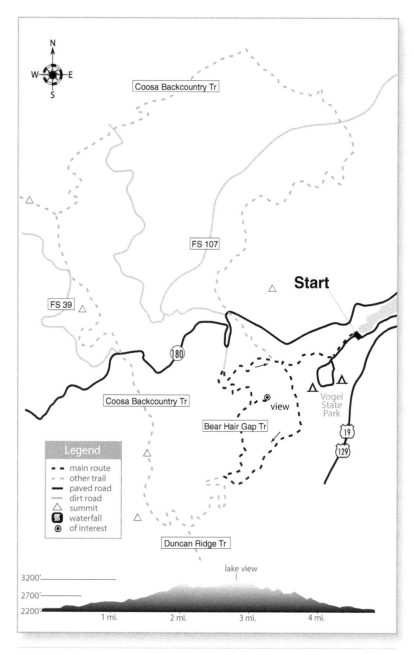

Coosa Backcountry Tr

FS 107

FS 39

Start

180

Coosa Backcountry Tr

view

Vogel State Park

Bear Hair Gap Tr

19

129

Legend

- ▬ ▬ main route
- ▬ ▬ other trail
- ▬ paved road
- ▬ dirt road
- △ summit
- ▓ waterfall
- ◉ of interest

Duncan Ridge Tr

lake view

3200'
2700'
2200'

1 mi. 2 mi. 3 mi. 4 mi.

🥾 Coosa Backcountry Trail

Hike Distance	14.6 miles
Type of Hike	Loop
Difficulty	Strenuous
Hiking Time	All Day
Start Elevation	2,330 ft
Total Ascent	4,715 ft
Land Manager	State Park
Fee	$5

A U.S. Geological Survey benchmark
is embedded in stone on the summit of
Coosa Bald.

This is probably the most difficult hike in this book. No matter what
the terrain, 14.6 miles is a long way to hike. Add to that a total ascent
of 4,715 feet and you've got the recipe for a seriously long day. This
particular trail was built with backpackers in mind—hikers who would
stretch the distance over two days or more. For those in good hiking
shape, it's certainly manageable in a day. Just make sure you get an
early start.

The route begins at Vogel State Park, where you'll need to stop in
at information desk and pick up a backcountry permit. A ranger will
ask you a few questions and answer any you may have before you go.
Then you're off on the hike which takes you well into the national forest.
First up is Sosebee Cove, a large drainage area for Wolf Creek known
for wildflowers. After crossing the creek you'll start a demanding four-
mile climb to the top of Coosa Bald, the highlight of the trip. You'll then
work your way up and down to Slaughter Gap on the flank of Blood
Mountain before finally looping back down to Vogel to end the day.

Getting to the Trailhead

The hike begins at Vogel State Park, located on US 19/129 south of Blairsville and north of Dahlonega. Park in the lake lot across from the visitor center and check-in station.

GPS Coordinates

N 34° 45.97′ W 83° 55.42′

★=Start

Hiking Directions

Begin First check in at the visitor center to obtain a hiking permit. Then walk up past cabin #7 to the trailhead.

Mile 0.2 Turn right onto the combined Bear Hair Gap/Coosa Backcountry Trail.

Mile 0.6 Turn right here to start the loop. You're still on the combined Bear Hair Gap/Coosa Backcountry Trail.

Mile 0.7 Bear right on the Coosa Backcountry Trail. Bear Hair Gap goes left.

Mile 1.3 Cross GA 180.

Mile 3.8 Cross footbridge over Wolf Creek, cross FS 107, and begin climbing.

Mile 6.4 Cross the dirt road at a large campsite.

Mile 7.6 Turn right on Duncan Ridge Trail. This is the spur to the Coosa Bald summit.

Mile 7.8 Reach summit of Coosa Bald. Views are spotty here unless the leaves are off the trees. Look for the benchmark at the highest point and take a break; you're just over halfway. Retrace your steps back down Duncan Ridge Trail.

Mile 8.0 Continue straight back onto the loop.

Mile 8.5 You'll bump into FS 39 but not cross it.

Mile 9.8 Cross GA 180 at Wolfpen Gap and begin climbing again on the far side.

Mile 11.6 Reach Slaughter Gap. Duncan Ridge Trail exits right here and climbs up to the Appalachian Trail on Blood Mountain. Bear left to stay on the loop.

Mile 12.6 Bear Hair Gap Trail enters from the left. Stay straight.

Mile 14.0 Complete the loop. Turn right and retrace your steps to the trailhead.

Mile 14.6 Finish.

Coosa Backcountry Trail Map

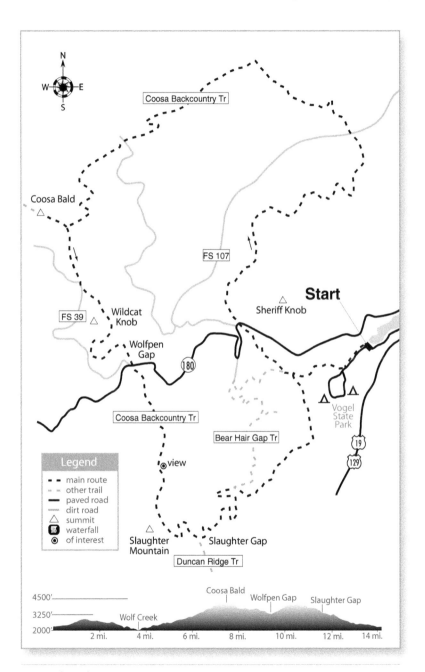

Legend
- - - main route
- - - other trail
—— paved road
—— dirt road
△ summit
▨ waterfall
◉ of interest

Coosa Backcountry Tr

Coosa Bald

FS 107

△ Start
Sheriff Knob

FS 39 △ Wildcat
Knob

Wolfpen
Gap

180

Coosa Backcountry Tr

Bear Hair Gap Tr

◉ view

△ Vogel
State
Park

19
129

△
Slaughter
Mountain   Slaughter Gap

Duncan Ridge Tr

4500' ____
Coosa Bald Wolfpen Gap Slaughter Gap
3250' ____
Wolf Creek
2000' ____
2 mi.   4 mi.   6 mi.   8 mi.   10 mi.   12 mi.   14 mi.

⚇ Slaughter Creek Loop

Hike Distance	8.2 miles
Type of Hike	Loop
Difficulty	Strenuous
Hiking Time	3/4 Day
Start Elevation	2,882 ft
Total Ascent	2092 ft
Land Manager	USFS
Fee	$3

The Appalachian Trail snakes silently through the woods near Jarrard Gap.

Climbing to the top of Blood Mountain is a rite of passage for hikers in north Georgia. Not only is it the highest summit on the Georgia section of the Appalachian Trail, but atop this rocky, windswept peak is a stone shelter built by the Civilian Conservation Corps in 1934. It's listed on the National Historic Register. You'll also find a outstanding views from the tops of a number of huge boulders there. One is known as Picnic Rock.

You'll approach Blood Mountain on this hike the same way northbound AT hikers do, from the southwest side—the easier route. Starting at Lake Winfield Scott, the circuit route follows Jarrard Gap Trail up to the gap where you'll pick up the AT. After that you'll skip through Horsebone, Turkey Stamp, and Bird Gaps before making the push up to the top of Blood Mountain. It's a good climb, but not extreme. Be sure to pack a lunch for Picnic Rock. After enjoying the views and checking out the shelter, retrace your steps up the mountain and take Slaughter Creek Trail back down to Lake Winfield Scott.

Getting to the Trailhead

The hike begins at Lake Winfield Scott Recreation Area Day Use Area. Follow GA 180 west from Vogel State Park for 6.2 miles. The trailhead parking is beside the lake.

GPS Coordinates
N 34° 44.37′ W 83° 58.49′

Hiking Directions

Begin Walk out beside the lake. When you reach the campground road, bear left and then cross and continue onto the trail.

Mile 0.2 Cross the creek and road, then turn left to stay on trail.

Mile 0.5 Cross footbridge and then turn right on a dirt road to begin the loop.

Mile 0.7 Bear right off dirt road onto Jarrard Gap Trail.

Mile 1.5 Reach Jarrard Gap. Turn left on the AT.

Mile 2.9 Freeman Trail enters from the right, and a trail to the

left goes to Woods Hole Shelter. Continue straight on the AT.

Mile 3.3 Slaughter Creek Trail exits here to the left. Stay on the AT and begin climbing Blood Mountain.

Mile 3.7 Duncan Ridge Trail enters from the left. Stay on the AT.

Mile 4.2 Reach summit of Blood Mountain. The shelter and picnic rock are just in front of you. Stay as long as you like, then retrace your steps to Slaughter Creek Trail.

Mile 6.2 Turn right on Slaughter Creek Trail.

Mile 7.7 Complete the loop. Turn right to return to the trailhead.

Mile 8.2 Finish.

The summit of Blood Mountain is often shrouded in a misty cloud.

Slaughter Creek Loop Trail Map

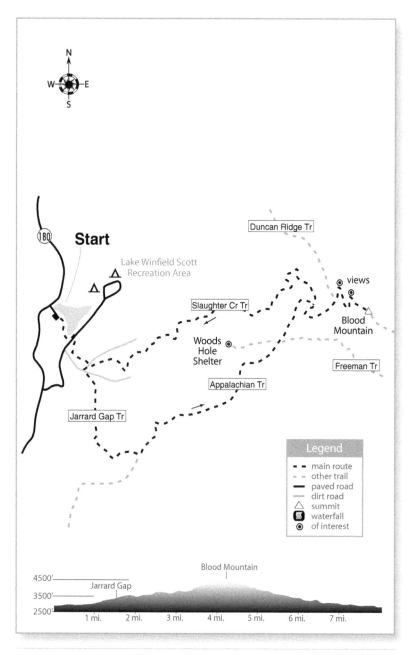

Blood Mountain Loop

From various spots on Blood Mountain the views in all directions are fabulous.

Hike Distance	6 miles
Type of Hike	Loop
Difficulty	Strenuous
Hiking Time	3/4 Day
Start Elevation	3,013 ft
Total Ascent	2,882 ft
Land Manager	USFS
Fee	None

From Neels Gap there are a couple of ways to get to the top of Blood Mountain. Many folks make the mistake of taking the most direct route—straight up the Appalachian Trail. That's the shortest way to go, but it certainly is not the easiest. This route has you circling the mountain first, coming up the back side. It's a little farther to walk, but the climb is not so extreme. Because you'll be walking a loop, there's something new to see around every bend in the trail.

Start your hike at the Byron Herbert Reece Trailhead. This is half a mile or so down the road, north of Neels Gap, where parking is limited and not allowed for long time periods. Take the Byron Herbert Reece Trail up to the AT, then circle the mountain via the Freeman Trail. By the time you reconnect with the AT, you've gained bit of altitude. The AT will take you up and over Blood Mountain. On top you'll find a historic stone shelter and views in all directions, the best one from a boulder called Picnic Rock. The return downhill hike is steep, and you'll walk over more large boulder slabs, so watch your step.

Getting to the Trailhead

From Neels Gap north of Dahlonega on US 19/129, drive 0.6 mile north to the Byron Herbert Reece trailhead on the left.

GPS Coordinates
N 34° 44.51' W 83° 55.37'

Hiking Directions

Begin Walk up Byron Herbert Reece trail.

Mile 0.8 Cross the AT onto Freeman Trail.

Mile 2.4 Turn right on the AT.

Mile 2.8 Slaughter Creek Trail enters from the left. Stay on AT.

Mile 3.2 Duncan Ridge Trail enters from the left. Stay on AT.

Mile 3.7 Top of Blood Mountain. There's a stone shelter here as well as some great vantage points from the boulders above.

Mile 5.2 Turn left on Byron Herbert Reece Trail.

Mile 6.0 Finish.

As it descends Blood Mountain, much of the Appalachian Trail is made up of large slabs of rock. Look for the trail blazes painted on the ground.

Blood Mountain Loop Trail Map

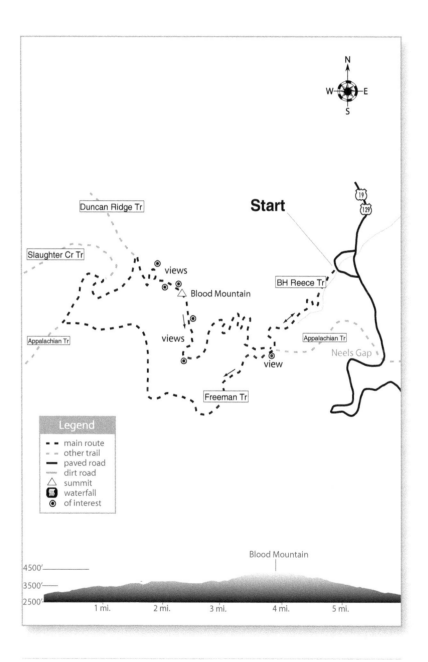

Start

Duncan Ridge Tr

Slaughter Cr Tr

views

△ Blood Mountain

BH Reece Tr

Appalachian Tr

views

Appalachian Tr

Neels Gap

view

Freeman Tr

Legend
- - main route
- - other trail
— paved road
— dirt road
△ summit
▦ waterfall
◉ of interest

Blood Mountain

4500'
3500'
2500'

1 mi.   2 mi.   3 mi.   4 mi.   5 mi.

⛰ Levelland Mountain View

Hike Distance	7.2 miles
Type of Hike	Out & Back
Difficulty	Moderate
Hiking Time	Half Day
Start Elevation	3,013 ft
Total Ascent	2,096 ft
Land Manager	USFS
Fee	None

At Neels Gap the Appalachian Trail goes right through the Mountain Crossings store.

Should you arrive at the trailhead ready to hike up Blood Mountain and find the parking lot packed with cars, not to worry. You can avoid the crowds and hike up to Levelland Mountain instead. This is the other direction to go on the Appalachian Trail from Neels Gap. The views from the top are pretty good, and you'll save your knees from the brutal Blood Mountain descent.

This hike begins from the Byron Herbert Reece Trailhead just north of Neels Gap. Hike up BHR Trail and turn left on the AT. Just down the trail are some interesting stacked boulders. At Neels Gap you'll get the chance to hike right through the Mountain Crossing store. Now's the time to buy a trail snack or the pair of trekking poles you've always wanted. Back on the trail, you'll make the steady climb up Levelland Mountain.

When you reach the summit, continue on over the top and a short distance down the other side to an awesome rock outcrop view. Look for Brasstown Bald to the northeast as well as Hogpen Gap and the spine of the Appalachians.

Getting to the Trailhead

From Neels Gap north of Dahlonega on US 19/129, drive 0.6 mile north to the Byron Herbert Reece trailhead on the left.

GPS Coordinates
N 34° 44.51′ W 83° 55.37′

Hiking Directions

Begin Walk up the Byron Herbert Reece Trail.

Mile 0.8 Turn left on the AT. There's a good view here to the south, and a little ways down the trail you should spot two large boulders, one stacked on of top the other.

Mile 1.7 Cross US 19/129 at Neels Gap. Continue up through Mountain Crossings. You might want to stop in at the store. Just beyond it is a nice viewing spot looking south. Once back on the AT, begin climbing Levelland Mountain.

Mile 3.4 There are two summits of Levelland Mountain. When you reach the second summit, continue over the top and down the far side.

Mile 3.6 Reach a rock outcrop view facing east. It's a nice place to sit down and take a break. After soaking in the view, retrace your steps to the trailhead.

Mile 7.2 Finish.

Imagine the forces it took to stack these two boulders.

Levelland Mountain View Trail Map

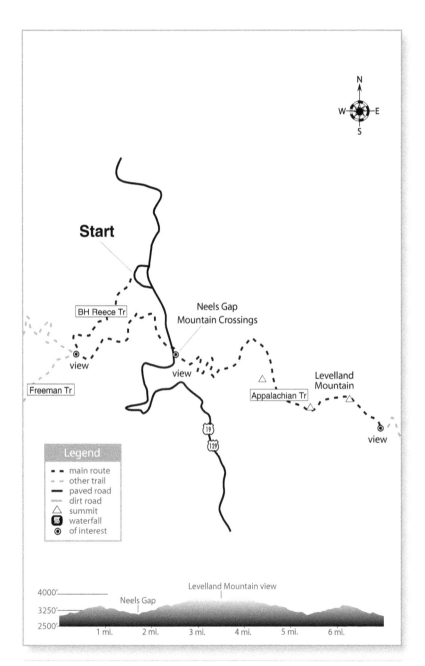

DAY HIKING THE NORTH GEORGIA MOUNTAINS

⚶ Desoto Falls Trail

The upper falls at Desoto Falls Scenic Area
is 100 feet high.

Hike Distance	2.5 miles
Type of Hike	T-shape
Difficulty	Easier
Hiking Time	2 hours
Start Elevation	2,088 ft
Total Ascent	415 ft
Land Manager	USFS
Fee	$3

If you like short hikes with big rewards, this one is for you. This well-used trail takes you out to two very pretty waterfalls. One is 40 feet high ,and the other is 100 feet high. There's an observation platform at each one with optimum views, so don't forget your camera. The hike begins by crossing over a wooden footbridge, after which you can turn left to the lower falls or right to the upper falls. It does not matter in which order you visit them, but by going to the lower falls first, you save the highest and most spectacular for last.

The area surrounding the tiny hamlet of Turners Corner is rich with waterfalls, and you're likely to run into waterfall buffs on most any trail. The falls at Desoto Falls Scenic Area are well known. A quiet picnic area is adjacent to the trailhead, and next door to that is a shady campground on the banks of Frogtown Creek. Many of the folks you'll see hiking are camping in the campground.

Getting to the Trailhead

From Dahlonega, drive north to Turners Corner on US 19. Continue another 5.0 miles north on US 19/129 to Desoto Falls Scenic Area. It's on the left side of the road before you reach Neels Gap. Park in the day-use parking lot.

GPS Coordinates
N 34° 42.39′ W 83° 54.92′

Hiking Directions

Begin From the day-use area, follow the trail down through the picnic area and around the lower edge of the campground. Cross the footbridge and turn left toward the lower falls.

Mile 0.4 Viewing platform for the lower falls. This a 40-foot tiered drop. Downstream about 50 yards is another 15-foot drop which you can see from the trail above. Turn back here and re-trace your steps to the main trail.

Mile 0.7 Back at the footbridge, continue straight on the trail following Frogtown Creek upstream.

Mile 1.4 Cross a branch of Frogtown Creek on a footbridge, then turn left toward the upper falls.

Mile 1.5 Viewing platform for the upper falls. This is a 100-foot multi-tiered drop. From here, turn around and head back to the trailhead the way you came.

Mile 2.3 Turn left to cross over the footbridge.

Mile 2.5 Finish.

Desoto Falls Trail Map

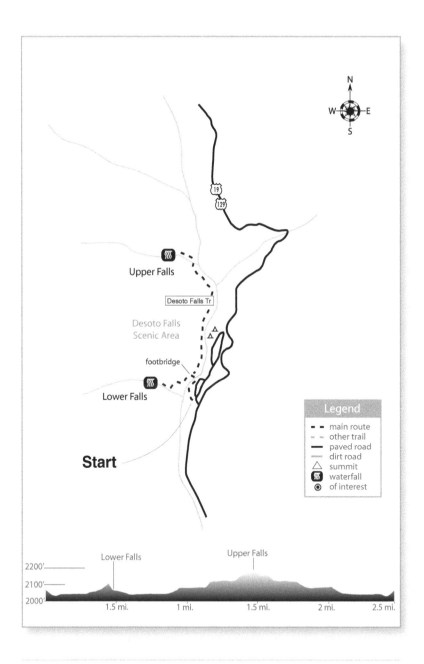

N
W—E
S

19
129

Upper Falls

Desoto Falls Tr

Desoto Falls
Scenic Area

footbridge

Lower Falls

Start

Legend
- - main route
- - other trail
— paved road
- dirt road
△ summit
🌊 waterfall
◉ of interest

Lower Falls   Upper Falls

2200'
2100'
2000'
1.5 mi.   1 mi.   1.5 mi.   2 mi.   2.5 mi.

Western Blue Ridge

Appalachian Trail Approach Trail

🥾 Dockery Lake Trail

Hike Distance	4.6 miles
Type of Hike	Out & Back
Difficulty	Moderate
Hiking Time	Half Day
Start Elevation	2,464 ft
Total Ascent	1,322 ft
Land Manager	USFS
Fee	None

You'll start and end this hike walking along the shores of Dockery Lake.

Finding a spectacular hidden waterfall is the culmination of this hike. The Dockery Lake Trail travels from Dockery Lake all the way up to the Appalachian Trail, but you'll stop short of that to do a little bushwhacking to a 200-foot falls on Pigeon Roost Creek. Since you'll be going a short way off-trail, pay special attention to the directions so you'll actually reach your goal.

Begin by walking down to and beside Dockery Lake. This pretty mountain lake can look very inviting on a warm day, so if it's summer and the weather is good, give yourself time for a swim on the return; you'll be ready to cool off by then. Soon the trail leaves the lake and circles around the mountain before going down to Pigeon Roost Creek. Once at the creek you'll follow an old roadbed up and away from the stream as you begin to climb again. Notice the stone walls on either side of the trail—imagine what it took to place them there. Soon you'll leave the trail behind to bushwhack over to Martha Falls on Pigeon Roost Creek.

Getting to the Trailhead

Take GA 60 north from Dahlonega for 15.0 miles and turn right into Dockery Lake Recreation Area. Continue down to the trailhead parking area near the lake.

GPS Coordinates

N 34° 40.39' W 83° 58.62'

Hiking Directions

Begin Walk down onto Dockery Lake Trail and head around the left side of the lake.

Mile 0.3 The dam will be just to your right. Bear left, following the sign indicating this trail leads to the AT. You can hear Dockery Creek crashing below.

Mile 2.0 Pay close attention here. The trail has been following an old roadbed lined with moss-covered stones. You'll cross two small streams within 0.2 mile. After crossing the second one, step off 100 paces and turn right off the trail and over the old wall, into the woods. Now walk at a right angle to

the trail, over the rise, and down toward Pigeon Roost Creek. If the stars have lined up correctly, you hold your teeth right, and you did not cheat on your taxes, you should see the waterfall right ahead of you. Good luck. After viewing the falls (or wandering around aimlessly), return the way you came on Dockery Lake Trail, back to the trailhead.

Mile 4.6 Finish.

The bottom portion of Martha Falls on Pigeon Roost Creek.

Dockery Lake Trail Map

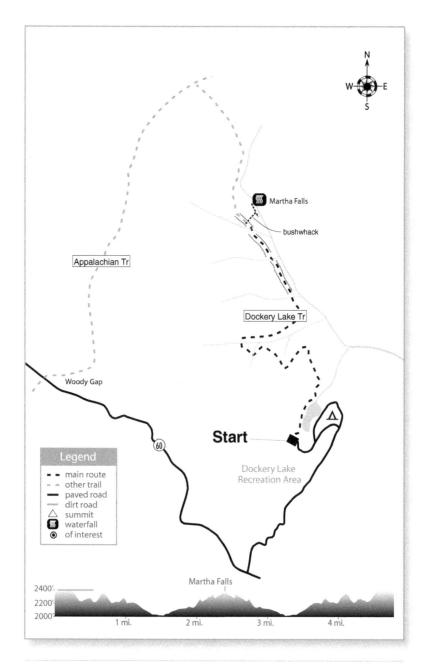

Martha Falls

bushwhack

Appalachian Tr

Dockery Lake Tr

Woody Gap

Start

60

Legend

- — main route
- — other trail
— paved road
〜 dirt road
△ summit
🌀 waterfall
◉ of interest

Dockery Lake
Recreation Area

2400'
2200'
2000'

Martha Falls

1 mi.   2 mi.   3 mi.   4 mi.

🥾 Preaching Rock View

Hike Distance	2.1 miles
Type of Hike	Out & Back
Difficulty	Easier
Hiking Time	2 hours
Start Elevation	3,164 ft
Total Ascent	430 ft
Land Manager	USFS
Fee	None

The view from Preaching Rock shows ridge after ridge in three directions.

Everyone loves a good view, and without too much difficulty or time commitment, that's what you get on this hike. Preaching Rock is the first good vantage point Appalachian Trail hikers reach when they enter the Blood Mountain Wilderness from the south. When you arrive, step up onto the rock and look out over the mountains. It's not too hard to imagine you're standing in a huge pulpit with a vast congregation spread out before you.

Woody Gap serves as the trailhead for the walk up to Preaching Rock. This is where GA 60 cuts through on its way north from Dahlonega to Suches. There's an overlook here and picnic tables. Your hike takes you north on the AT for just over a mile, the last 0.3 mile a fairly steep climb to the top of a cliff and then on to Preaching Rock. Given its proximity to the road and the short distance, this is a popular hike, so don't expect too much solitude. You might consider packing a picnic, either to eat at the Woody Gap tables or on Preaching Rock itself.

Getting to the Trailhead

The trailhead is located at Woody Gap on GA 60, 2.0 miles south of Suches and 14.0 miles north of Dahlonega.

GPS Coordinates

N 34° 40.66′ W 83° 59.98′

★=Start

Hiking Directions

Begin Walk across GA 60 and north on the AT.

Mile 0.9 Arrive at a clifftop vantage point with excellent views toward Dahlonega and the southwest.

Mile 1.0+ Reach Preaching Rock. It's unmistakable. Notice a tiny campsite here as well. After soaking in the views and getting a bit of a rest, head back the way you came.

Mile 2.1 Finish.

Woody Gap Trailhead boasts a picnic area with a view.

Preaching Rock View Trail Map

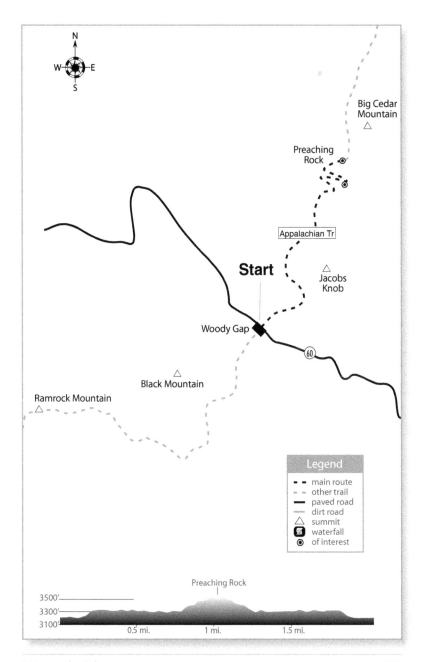

Legend
- - main route
- - other trail
━ paved road
— dirt road
△ summit
waterfall
◉ of interest

🥾 Woody Gap Ramble

Hike Distance	2.8 miles
Type of Hike	Out & Back
Difficulty	Easier
Hiking Time	3 hours
Start Elevation	3,160 ft
Total Ascent	630 ft
Land Manager	USFS
Fee	None

The Appalachian Trail near Woody Gap starts out nice and level.

It's hard to find flat sections of the Appalachian Trail in north Georgia. Most access points are from road crossings at various gaps. By its very nature, a gap is a low spot between ridges, and the hiker starting out from one often encounters a steep climb right from the start. However, this is not the case when you walk south on the AT from Woody Gap. For close to a mile the trail undulates only slightly. Compared with most hikes on the AT, it feels like a walk in the park. For this reason, plus the fact that a short climb at the end takes you up to a good view spot, this is a friendly, satisfying sort of hike that many people can enjoy without too much difficulty.

As soon as you leave Woody Gap and head south, the woods close in around you, and the trail feels as remote as if you were miles from nowhere. Before long you'll pass by a seeping waterfall that drips and gurgles from high above you to right under your feet. Eventually you'll work your way out to the far end of a low saddle where a short, steep climb takes you up to a rock outcrop viewpoint.

Getting to the Trailhead

The trailhead is located at Woody Gap on GA 60, 2.0 miles south of Suches and 14.0 miles north of Dahlonega.

GPS Coordinates
N 34° 40.66' W 83° 59.98'

Hiking Directions

Begin Walk south on the AT.

Mile 0.4 A small waterfall cascades onto the trail here.

Mile 0.6 Here look for a small spring on the right side of the trail.

Mile 1.4 Cross a low saddle and hike up a short but steep pitch to reach a rock outcrop. After enjoying the view, retrace your steps to Woody Gap.

Mile 2.8 Finish.

What Exactly is a Gap?

How many gaps do you see in this photo?

In the South, we call it a gap. In the northeast, it's known as a notch. Out west, you'd call the same thing a pass. Sometimes it takes the form of a saddle or a swag. In Wales it's called a *bwich,* and the Gaelic word for it is *bealach.* What exactly *is* it?

A gap is a low spot in a ridgeline of mountains. Nowadays, the most well-known gaps are typically the lowest spots where main roads cut through the mountains. You can bet that in the old days, native American trails or wagon roads passed through them as well. Hiking the Appalachian Trail in north Georgia, you could easily pass through ten or more gaps in a day. Since you're walking a ridgeline, just about every time you go down, you pass through a gap.

Woody Gap Ramble Trail Map

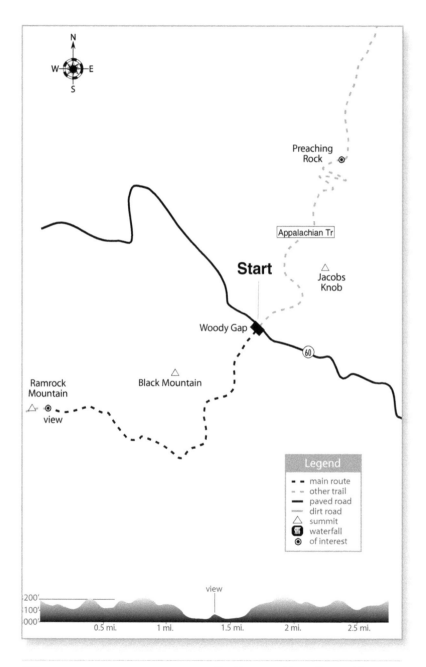

Preaching
Rock ◉

Appalachian Tr

Start

△
Jacobs
Knob

Woody Gap ◆

60

△
Black Mountain

Ramrock
Mountain
△ ◉
view

Legend
- ▬ ▬ main route
- – – other trail
- ▬▬ paved road
- ─── dirt road
- △ summit
- ♨ waterfall
- ◉ of interest

view

200'
100'
000'

0.5 mi.   1 mi.   1.5 mi.   2 mi.   2.5 mi.

Sassafras Mountain View

Hike Distance	2.4 miles
Type of Hike	Out & Back
Difficulty	Moderate
Hiking Time	3 hours
Start Elevation	2,844 ft
Total Ascent	744 ft
Land Manager	USFS
Fee	None

In some places on Sassafras Mountain, the view is through a gap in the trees.

Should you find yourself driving around on the high dirt roads north of Dahlonega and in need of a leg stretcher, give this hike a try. Be aware that the basis for the difficulty rating on this hike is not distance. The climb on the Appalachian Trail from Cooper Gap is anything but easy; in fact it's pretty darn steep. So, even though you only hike a little over two miles, it will feel like much more. If you take it easy on the climb and watch your step on the way back down, you shouldn't have too much trouble.

Once you top out on the ridge of this hike, you'll find a beautiful stretch of trail. A host of wildflowers are in bloom spring, summer, and fall. May, in particular, offers a huge display of mayapple. Look for the big-leaf-on-a-stalk plants with the solitary white flower hanging below the leaf. At just over a half-mile and again at a little over a mile you'll come to two rock outcrop viewpoints with good views to the south, east, and west. Both spots are nice places to linger a while before returning to Cooper Gap.

Getting to the Trailhead

From downtown Dahlonega, go 2.2 miles north on US 19B. Turn left on Wahsega Road. Go 8.5 miles and turn right on FS 80 at Camp Frank Merrill. It's 2.2 miles farther to Cooper Gap and the trailhead.

GPS Coordinates
N 34° 39.19' W 84° 05.06'

Hiking Directions

Begin Walk south on the AT. Almost immediately you will be hiking up a steep mountainside.

Mile 0.6 Reach first rock outcrop view. Continue south on the AT from here.

Mile 1.2 Reach second rock outcrop view. When you are ready, retrace your steps from here.

Mile 2.4 Finish.

A large carpet of mayapple blooms on both sides of the Appalachian Trail atop Sassafras Mountain.

Sassafras Mountain View Trail Map

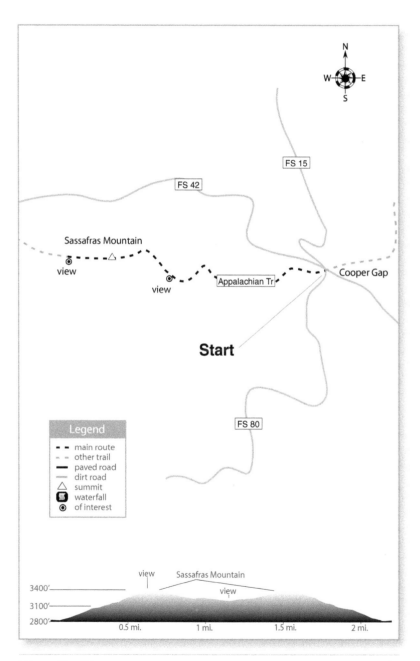

⚘ Brawley Mountain Firetower

Hike Distance	6 miles
Type of Hike	Loop
Difficulty	Moderate
Hiking Time	Half Day
Start Elevation	2,426 ft
Total Ascent	1,500 ft
Land Manager	USFS
Fee	None

A white diamond blaze marks the turn as the Benton MacKaye Trail sweeps past the Brawley Mountain Firetower.

Years ago, firetowers sprouted from many of the highest mountaintops in north Georgia where watchers kept constant vigil, always on the lookout for signs of wildfire. Today, in the era of satellites and other high-end technology, count yourself lucky if you come upon a tower still standing. Some, including the Brawley Mountain firetower, are now used to attach radio, TV, and cell transmitters. It's changed their look from that of a lonesome outpost to a mega-voltage superstructure. And like many other firetowers today, the one at Brawley Mountain is closed to visitors.

On this hike you'll walk along a section of the Benton MacKaye Trail from Wilscot Gap to the top of Brawley Mountain. The trail on the way up passes through a rich cove forest where in spring there's a marvelous display of wildflowers. You'll also pass over the top of Tipson Mountain and over Bald Top, which is no longer bald. Upon reaching the tower you'll leave the trail behind and return to the trailhead via the tower access road. This gated dirt road offers dramatic views to the southeast all along its way.

Getting to the Trailhead

From Morganton, travel south on GA 60 for 7.6 miles to where Benton MacKaye Trail crosses the road at Wilscot Gap. Or from Suches, travel 20.4 miles north to the same gap.

GPS Coordinates
N 34° 48.47' W 84° 11.25'

Hiking Directions

Begin Walk across the road and onto Benton MacKaye Trail.

Mile 1.2 A short side trail on the left here connects with FS 45. Stay on Benton MacKaye.

Mile 2.4 Reach Ledford Gap, where you'll connect with FS 45. Go right and then right again, back onto the foot trail.

Mile 3.2 A short side trail to the left connects to FS 45. Stay on Benton MacKaye.

Mile 3.4 Reach the summit of Brawley Mountain and the firetower. You'll return from here to the trailhead via FS 45.

Mile 4.1 Ledford Gap. Stay on FS 45.

Mile 6.0 Finish.

The summit of Brawley Mountain offers spotty views.

Brawley Mountain Firetower Trail Map

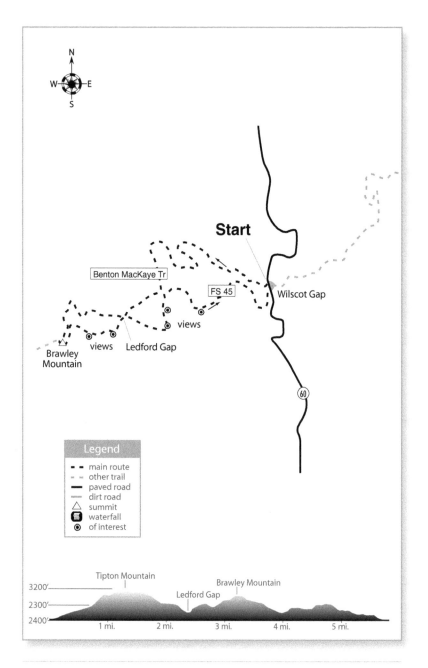

N
W E
S

Start

Benton MacKaye Tr

FS 45

Wilscot Gap

views

views   Ledford Gap

Brawley
Mountain

60

Legend
- - main route
- - other trail
— paved road
— dirt road
△ summit
🌊 waterfall
◉ of interest

Tipton Mountain

Brawley Mountain

3200'

Ledford Gap

2300'
2400'
1 mi.   2 mi.   3 mi.   4 mi.   5 mi.

⚐ Deadennen Mountain View

Hike Distance	3.4 miles
Type of Hike	Out & Back
Difficulty	Moderate
Hiking Time	3 hours
Start Elevation	2,426 ft
Total Ascent	930 ft
Land Manager	USFS
Fee	None

The Benton MacKaye Trail heads up Deadennen Mountain on its way north to Skeenah Gap.

Hikers who've taken the walk up to Brawley Mountain firetower might be interested to know what's in the other direction on the Benton MacKaye Trail. Here's what you'll find. The trail heads almost due east from Wilscot Gap and soon ascends Deadennen Mountain. Should you be hiking at a time of year when there are no leaves on the trees, the views are pretty good. Once warmer weather sets in and the trees are leafed out, the views get spotty at best. Look around, though; you'll be hiking through a white pine and oak forest. In May this is the perfect time to look for pink lady's slippers. This exotic-looking native wildflower loves the acidic soil formed from the acid leaching out of the fallen pine needles.

From the trailhead, you'll hike up and over a small knob to Lula Head Gap. Who knows what (or who) a "lula head" is? From there, where an old forest road ends, you'll begin the climb up Deadennen Mountain. Watch closely—the trail used to go straight up, but now it switchbacks up the mountain. You can still see traces of the old trail. Once at the summit, take a break and then return to the trailhead.

Getting to the Trailhead

From Morganton, travel south on GA 60 for 7.6 miles to where the Benton MacKaye Trail crosses the road at Wilscot Gap. From Suches, travel 20.4 miles north to the same gap.

GPS Coordinates
N 34° 48.47' W 84° 11.25'

Hiking Directions

Begin Walk east on the Benton MacKaye Trail. This is the same side of the road you are parked on.

Mile 0.9 Cross end of FS 640A and begin ascent of Deadennen Mountain.

Mile 1.7 Reach summit of Deadennen Mountain. From here, retrace your steps to the trailhead.

Mile 3.4 Finish.

Pink lady's slippers thrive in acidic soils formed by decomposing pine needles.

Deadennen Mountain View Trail Map

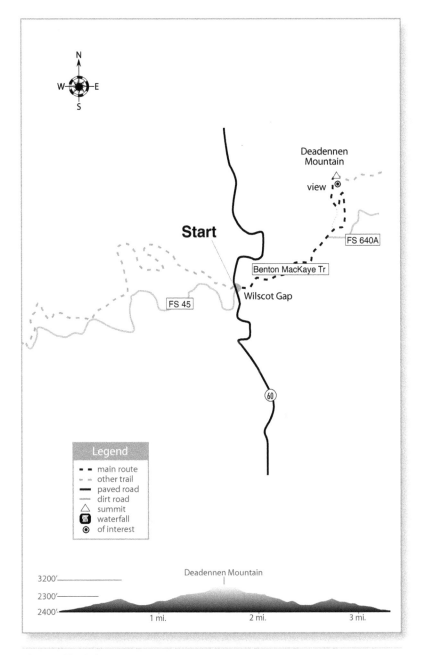

Start

Deadennen Mountain

view

FS 640A

Benton MacKaye Tr

Wilscot Gap

FS 45

60

Legend
- – – main route
- – – other trail
- — paved road
- — dirt road
- △ summit
- 🌊 waterfall
- ◉ of interest

Deadennen Mountain

3200'
2300'
2400'

1 mi.   2 mi.   3 mi.

⚡ Wallalah Mountain View

Hike Distance	3.4 miles
Type of Hike	Out & Back
Difficulty	Moderate
Hiking Time	3 hours
Start Elevation	2,024 ft
Total Ascent	1,000 ft
Land Manager	USFS
Fee	None

You'll cross this bridge over a bold stream just after leaving the trailhead.

Sometimes all you want to do is walk up to a nice view of the surrounding countryside without having to drive all over that countryside to get there. The hike up Wallalah Mountain is just this sort trip. It's not far from Suches and right on GA 60, a very curvy, scenic highway which travels between Dahlonega and Blue Ridge. The hike up the mountain along the Benton MacKaye Trail is steep enough to get your blood pumping, but not so long that your legs will give out before you finish.

The Benton MacKaye Trail crosses GA 60 in two places. You'll start at the first spot it crosses after leaving Springer Mountain. At this point it is also combined with the Duncan Ridge Trail. These two, plus the Appalachian Trail, the Bartram Trail, and the Pinhoti Trail make up the five long distance foot trails in north Georgia. From the trailhead, the route goes up almost from the very beginning. At just over 1.5 miles you'll come to a large rock outcrop where things open up for a fantastic view of the Appalachian ridges and the Cooper Creek valley where farm fields lie quietly in the shadows.

Getting to the Trailhead

From Morganton travel south on GA 60 for 11.9 miles to where the Benton MacKaye Trail crosses the road. From Suches travel 16.1 miles north to the same spot.

GPS Coordinates
N 34° 45.98' W 84° 09.84'

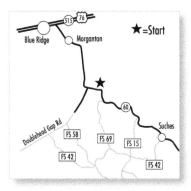

Hiking Directions

Begin Walk onto the Benton MacKaye/Duncan Ridge Trail down and across the creek on the footbridge.

Mile 0.7 A number of unmarked trails junction here with the trail you are following. Stay on the white diamond blazed Benton MacKaye/Duncan Ridge Trail.

Mile 1.7 Reach summit of Wallalah Mountain. Here you'll find a rock outcrop with a big view. After you've gotten your heart rate back down and enjoyed the view, return the way you came up.

Mile 3.4 Finish.

Who Was Benton MacKaye?

A memorial to Benton MacKaye atop Springer Mountain.

There's good reason that both the Appalachian Trail and the Benton MacKaye Trail have their southern terminus on north Georgia's Springer Mountain. Benton MacKaye was the person who inspired the idea for the Appalachian Trail. He was a forestry teacher at Harvard, an employee of the U.S. Forest Service, and a founding member of the Wilderness Society. He worked diligently to ensure that future generations would have a trail that was "rigorously maintained and not allowed to revert to disuse." The Benton MacKaye Trail continues from Springer Mountain for close to 300 miles, all the way to Davenport Gap on the northern border of the Great Smoky Mountains National Park. It follows part of the route that Benton MacKaye originally proposed for the Appalachian Trail.

Wallalah Mountain View Trail Map

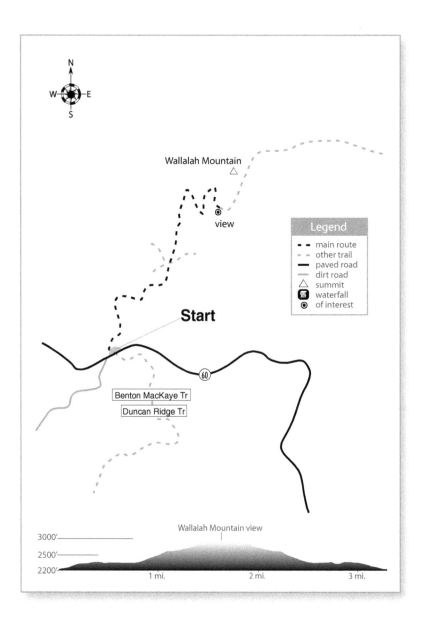

Wallalah Mountain

view

Start

Benton MacKaye Tr
Duncan Ridge Tr

60

Legend
- - main route
- - other trail
— paved road
— dirt road
△ summit
▨ waterfall
◉ of interest

Wallalah Mountain view

3000'
2500'
2200'
1 mi.   2 mi.   3 mi.

⚐ Toccoa River Bridge

Hike Distance	7.4 miles
Type of Hike	Out & Back
Difficulty	Moderate
Hiking Time	3/4 Day
Start Elevation	2,024 ft
Total Ascent	1,896 ft
Land Manager	USFS
Fee	None

Your destination is this suspension footbridge where it crosses the Toccoa River.

Tourist information sheets list the remote footbridge crossing the Toccoa River near the Cooper Creek area as an interesting destination. And if you followed the directions, you'd drive there on a long and bumpy dirt road. But why do that when you can hike there instead, from a good trailhead on a paved road? The bridge *was* built as a way for hikers walking the Benton MacKaye/Duncan Ridge Trail to cross the wide and fast-flowing Toccoa River. Its status as a tourist destination is secondary. And don't worry, not very many people brave the long dirt road.

From the trailhead along GA 60 south of Morganton, you'll hike along the combined Benton MacKaye/Duncan Ridge Trail up to and along the ridge of Tooni Mountain. The entire length runs through a mixed hardwood forest, and once on the ridge you'll walk up and down gentle rises before dropping down gradually to the Toccoa River. You'll find the suspension footbridge here. The river is beautiful as it rolls through a long pool above the bridge and splashes through rapids just below—a great spot to take a break.

Getting to the Trailhead

From Morganton, travel south on GA 60 for 11.9 miles to where Benton MacKaye Trail crosses the road. From Suches, travel 16.1 miles north to the same spot.

GPS Coordinates
N 34° 45.98′ W 84° 09.84′

Hiking Directions

Begin Walk across the road and onto the Benton MacKaye/ Duncan Ridge Trail.

Mile 3.3 Cross straight over an old woods road.

Mile 3.7 Reach the suspension footbridge. This is a very nice spot. After taking a break, eating lunch, and/or swimming, return to the trailhead the way you came.

Mile 7.4 Finish.

Small rapids just below the bridge over the Toccoa River.

Toccoa River Bridge Trail Map

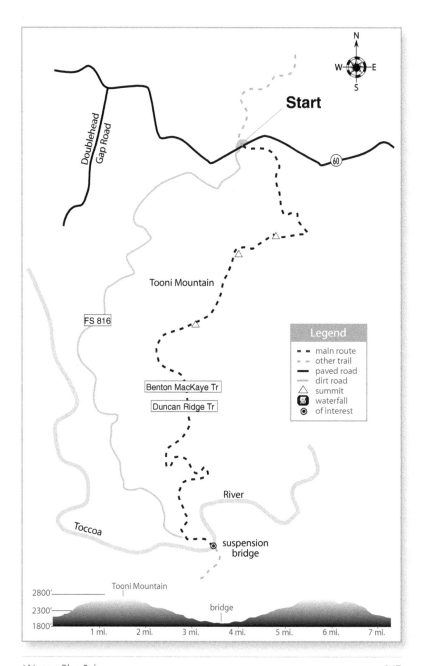

🚶🚶 Rich Mountain Loop

Hike Distance	4.8 miles
Type of Hike	Loop
Difficulty	Moderate
Hiking Time	Half Day
Start Elevation	2,550 ft
Total Ascent	980 ft
Land Manager	USFS
Fee	None

The trail across Rich Mountain passes through delightful woods.

Finding loop routes along the Appalachian Trail in north Georgia is a trick. Right near the AT's southern terminus at Springer Mountain, there are two. This one begins at an area known as Three Forks. It's where Chester Fork, Stover Creek, and Long Creek all meet to form Noontootla Creek. It's also where the AT and Benton MacKaye Trail merge for a while to share the same path.

For this route, you'll walk on the AT alongside Stover Creek for the first half of the loop and then return over the flanks of Rich Mountain on Benton MacKaye Trail. It's a very pretty hike. As you walk along the AT, you'll be heading upstream beside the creek. The farther you go, the smaller the stream gets. It's finally little more than a trickle as you head up into a rich cove forest, the type known for magnificent displays of wildflowers. Before you leave the AT altogether, be sure to take the side trail out to the Stover Creek shelter. It's a good place to take a break, and you might get a chance to talk with some backpackers.

Getting to the Trailhead

From the junction of Highway 515 and GA 60 just north of Blue Ridge, drive 13 miles on GA 60 and turn right on Doublehead Gap Road. Continue another 5.8 miles and turn left on FS 58. From here it is 3.2 miles to Noontootla Falls and 5.6 miles to Three Forks. You'll find the trailhead where the AT crosses the road.

GPS Coordinates
N 34° 39.80' W 84° 11.04

Hiking Directions

Begin Walk south, across the footbridge and onto the Appalachian/Benton MacKaye Trail.

Mile 0.1 Continue on AT as Benton MacKaye Trail exits to the left.

Mile 1.6 A blue-blazed trail on the left leads 0.1 miles to the Stover Creek Shelter. Be sure to check it out before continuing on the route.

Mile 2.6 Turn left on Benton MacKaye Trail.

Mile 4.7 Turn right as you rejoin the AT.

Mile 4.8 Finish.

Appalachian Trail thru-hikers prepare a late breakfast at Stover Creek shelter.

Rich Mountain Loop Trail Map

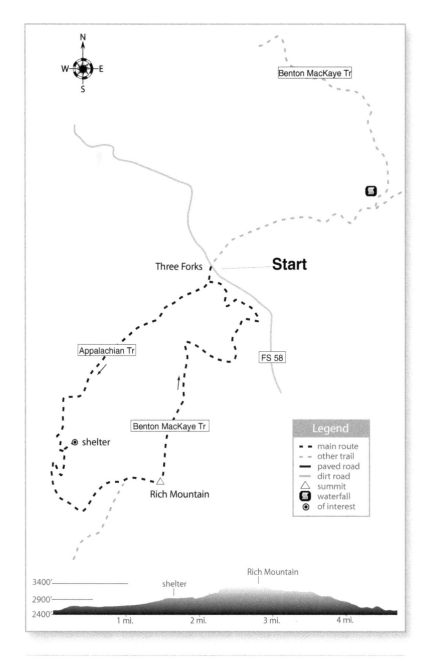

🥾 Long Creek Falls

Hike Distance	4.6 miles
Type of Hike	Out & Back
Difficulty	Moderate
Hiking Time	Half Day
Start Elevation	2,550 ft
Total Ascent	720 ft
Land Manager	USFS
Fee	None

Lunch break at Long Creek Falls.

Not many places exist along the Appalachian Trail in north Georgia where you can take a much-needed break alongside a sizeable waterfall. Long Creek Falls, just north of Three Forks, is one of those places. Most northbound Appalachian Trail thru-hikers encounter this spot on day one of their months-long expedition. Imagine leaving Springer Mountain in the morning and stopping at these falls for lunch!

On this route, you'll hike out to Long Creek Falls and then continue on to a large meadow high on a hill with a great view looking back south toward Springer Mountain. The hike starts at Three Forks and heads north along the combined AT/Benton MacKaye Trail. For the first mile or so you'll follow Long Creek. There are two more waterfalls on the creek before you get to the trail leading out to Long Creek Falls; you can hear them crashing down in the rhododendron. After viewing Long Creek Falls, you'll continue along Benton MacKaye Trail where a steep climb takes you up to your destination, the meadow view.

Getting to the Trailhead

From the junction of Highway 515 and GA 60 just north of Blue Ridge, drive 13 miles on GA 60 and turn right on Doublehead Gap Road. Continue another 5.8 miles and turn left on FS 58. From here it is 3.2 miles to Noontootla Falls and 5.6 miles to Three Forks. You'll find the trailhead where the AT crosses the road.

GPS Coordinates
N 34° 39.80' W 84° 11.04'

Hiking Directions

Begin Walk north on the AT/Benton MacKaye Trail.

Mile 0.8 Turn left here on the side trail to walk 0.1 mile to the base of Long Creek Falls. After visiting the falls, return to this spot and turn onto the Benton MacKaye/Duncan Ridge Trail. This is the southern terminus of the Duncan Ridge Trail. This trail will take you up beside the top of Long Creek Falls.

Mile 1.4 Bear left across a plank bridge to remain on the trail.

Mile 2.4 A short but steep climb brings you up to a large meadow with views of surrounding mountains. It's the kind of place that makes you want to spread out a blanket and take a nap. After your time here, retrace your steps (skipping the waterfall excursion) to the trailhead.

Mile 4.6 Finish.

Go ahead—kick off your shoes, spread a blanket, and stay awhile.

Long Creek Falls Trail Map

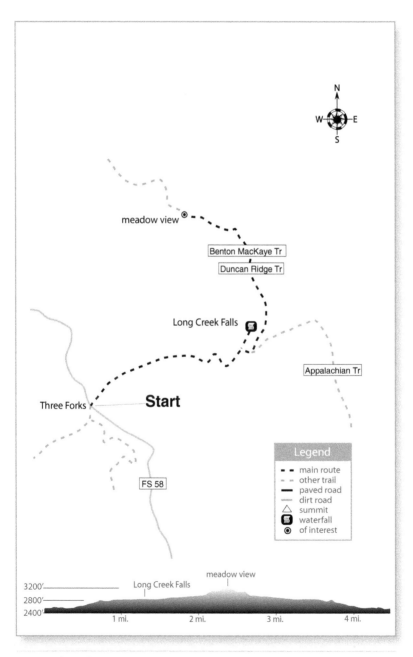

meadow view

Benton MacKaye Tr
Duncan Ridge Tr

Long Creek Falls

Appalachian Tr

Three Forks **Start**

FS 58

Legend
- - main route
- - other trail
— paved road
dirt road
△ summit
🌊 waterfall
◉ of interest

3200'
2800'
2400'

Long Creek Falls

meadow view

1 mi.   2 mi.   3 mi.   4 mi.

🚶 Springer Mountain Loop

Hike Distance	5.1 miles
Type of Hike	Loop
Difficulty	Moderate
Hiking Time	Half Day
Start Elevation	3,372 ft
Total Ascent	1,065 ft
Land Manager	USFS
Fee	None

The first white blaze of thousands lies atop Springer Mountain beside a plaque at the southern terminus of the Appalachian Trail.

For Appalachian Trail enthusiasts there are two mountains more important than all the rest. One is Maine's Mt. Katahdin, which marks the trails northern terminus; the other is Georgia's Springer Mountain, the southern terminus and the jumping off point for the vast majority of the roughly 2,000 hikers who attempt the entire AT each year. Neither of these mountains is easy to get to. You certainly can't drive up them. Foot travel is the only way, and that is no piece of cake.

On this hike you'll walk up Springer Mountain via the Benton MacKaye Trail, which also has its southern terminus here. Before reaching Springer, you'll cross the top of Ball Mountain with its inspiring clifftop view. Soon you'll turn onto the AT and climb to the very summit of Springer. It's a neat spot. On a large rock outcrop are several plaques and the southernmost white blaze—a stripe of white paint that for over 2,000 miles takes on an identity of its own, becoming many a hiker's friend on the trek north. Enjoy the views from the rock, and be sure to check out the hikers' log in the nearby shelter.

Getting to the Trailhead

From the junction of Highway 515 and GA 60 just north of Blue Ridge, drive 13.0 miles on GA 60 and turn right on Doublehead Gap Road. Continue another 5.8 miles and turn left on FS 58. Drive 5.9 miles to FS 42-3, turn right and go 2.7 miles. You'll find the trailhead where the AT crosses the road.

GPS Coordinates
N 34° 38.26' W 84° 11.70'

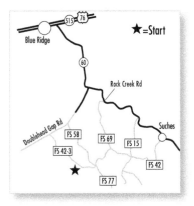

Hiking Directions

Begin Walk north on the AT.

Mile 0.3 Turn right on Benton MacKaye Trail.

Mile 1.7 Cross FS 42-3.

Mile 2.0 Turn left on the spur to the clifftop view on Ball Mountain.

Mile 3.5 Pass the Benton Mac-

Kaye Memorial, then turn left on the AT.

Mile 3.8 Springer Mountain summit. Check out the view and the plaques, then head back down the trail. Turn right to check out the shelter before continuing on down the mountain on the AT.

Mile 5.1 Finish.

Checking out the view from Ball Mountain cliff.

Springer Mountain Loop Trail Map

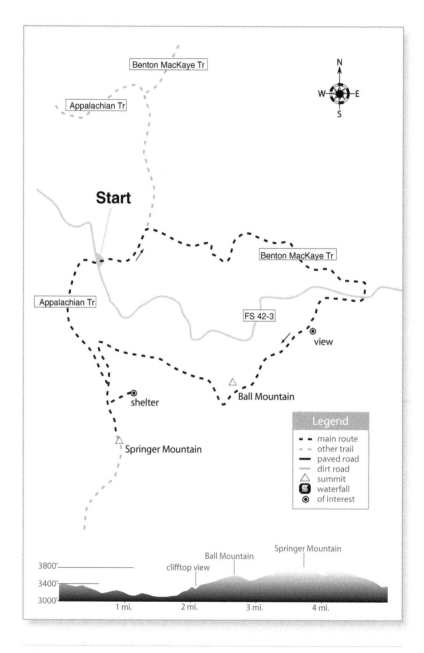

Benton MacKaye Tr

Appalachian Tr

Start

Benton MacKaye Tr

Appalachian Tr

FS 42-3

view

shelter

Ball Mountain

Springer Mountain

Legend

- - main route
- - other trail
— paved road
— dirt road
△ summit
🌊 waterfall
◉ of interest

Springer Mountain

Ball Mountain

clifftop view

3800'
3400'
3000'

1 mi.   2 mi.   3 mi.   4 mi.

🥾 Amicalola Falls Loop

Hike Distance	2.5 miles
Type of Hike	Loop
Difficulty	Moderate
Hiking Time	2 hours
Start Elevation	1,841 ft
Total Ascent	803 ft
Land Manager	State Park
Fee	$5

Be prepared to walk up more than 600 steps to reach the top of Amicalola Falls.

Amicalola Falls is north Georgia's highest waterfall, and at 729 feet, it's the third highest in the eastern United States. What a great place to hike! Note that this hike is similar to the ones at Cloudland Canyon State Park to the west and Tallulah Gorge State Park to the east. A series of wooden steps it takes you 0.3 mile, right up the face of the waterfall. At times water is splashing all around you, though you don't get wet.

The hike starts at the hikers' trailhead parking lot just in front of the park visitor center. You'll walk up past the reflecting pool where, when the water is still, you get a mirror image of the falls. Then it's on up the steps. Don't be surprised if you see backpackers heading up with heavy loads; this is also the beginning of the Appalachian Trail Approach Trail. Hikers start here to make the day-long hike up to Springer Mountain and southern terminus of the AT. Once up on top, the trail crosses over the very brink of the falls, where you can look straight down at the cascading water or outward for a top-of-Georgia view. To get back down, you'll loop around for a more gradual descent via the East Ridge Trail.

Getting to the Trailhead

Park and start at the hikers' trailhead parking lot in front of the information center, just beyond the entrance in Amicalola Falls State Park. The state park is between Ellijay and Dahlonega on GA 52.

GPS Coordinates
N 34° 33.50' W 84° 14.97'

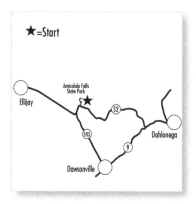

★=Start

Hiking Directions

Begin Hike up the blue-blazed AT Approach Trail, which begins directly behind the visitor center.

Mile 0.6 Pass the reflecting pool. Facing the falls with the pool in between, you should be able to see an inverted image of the waterfall.

Mile 0.75 Here begins a series of 175 steps, taking you up and over the bottom tiers of the waterfall.

Mile 0.95 The first set of steps ends at a bridge over the falls. It offers a great view of the top

section. Just ahead you'll turn to the right and continue up the last 425 steps.

Mile 1.2 Top of the falls. Bear right across the platform overlooking the lip of the falls and walk up to the upper parking lot toilets, where you'll turn right and head off the side of the mountain on East Ridge Trail. At this point it is an old roadbed.

Mile 1.8 Bear right off the roadbed as East Ridge Trail continues on a foot trail.

Mile 2.4 Close the loop where the trails meet behind the visitor center.

Mile 2.5 Finish back at the hikers' trailhead parking lot.

Open views at the start of East Ridge Trail.

Amicalola Falls Loop Trail Map

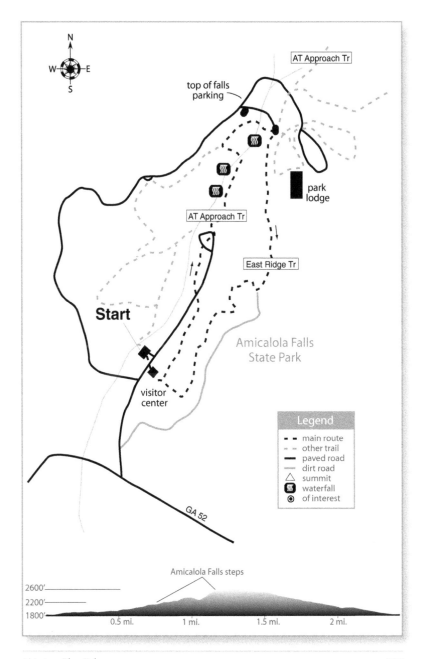

🏃 AT Approach Loop

Hike Distance	10.1 miles
Type of Hike	Loop
Difficulty	Strenuous
Hiking Time	All Day
Start Elevation	2,523 ft
Total Ascent	2,355 ft
Land Manager	State Park
Fee	$5

The Len Foote Hike Inn Lodge makes a great spot to stop for lunch or a break.

Just to get to the start of the Appalachian Trail at its southern terminus requires a strenuous eight-mile hike to the top of Springer Mountain. The lead-in trail is known simply as the Approach Trail, and it starts at Amicalola Falls State Park. The state park has another distinction; it has the only "hike-in" lodge in the state. If you're a guest, the only way to get to the lodge is on foot. The trail to the lodge and the trail leading to Springer Mountain comprise the AT Approach Loop.

In order to skip the tedious 600-step ascent and descent next to Amicalola Falls, you'll start this hike at the trailhead parking lot for hikers at the top of the falls. You'll do the loop counterclockwise by taking the trail to the lodge first; it near the halfway point, so it makes a good place to stop for lunch (unless you are a guest, you'll need to bring your own). Beyond the lodge, the AT climbs over Frosty Mountain. You can check out the remains of a lookout tower on top before returning to the state park.

Getting to the Trailhead

Park and start at the trailhead parking lot at the top of the falls in Amicalola Falls State Park, between Ellijay and Dahlonega on GA 52.

GPS Coordinates
N 34° 34.04' W 84° 14.61'

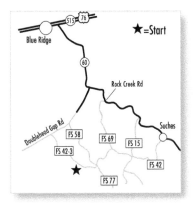

Hiking Directions

Begin Follow the AT Approach/Hike Inn Trail out of the top of the parking lot. The Approach Trail is blue-blazed and Hike Inn Trail is green-blazed.

Mile 0.3 Turn right on Hike Inn Trail to start the loop.

Mile 0.9 From a set of benches here, there is a nice view.

Mile 4.9 Reach Len Foote Hike Inn Lodge, which has excellent views from the porch. From here the trail continues on the far side of the inn entrance.

Mile 5.9 Turn left on the AT Approach Trail.

Mile 6.5 Reach the top of Frosty Mountain. You'll see the remains of a firetower here.

Mile 8.1 Cross a dirt road.

Mile 9.6 Cross a dirt road again, and then a footbridge.

Mile 9.8 Complete the loop. Retrace your steps to the trailhead.

Mile 10.1 Finish.

Here the AT Approach Trail travels through a mixed hardwood forest.

AT Approach Loop Trail Map

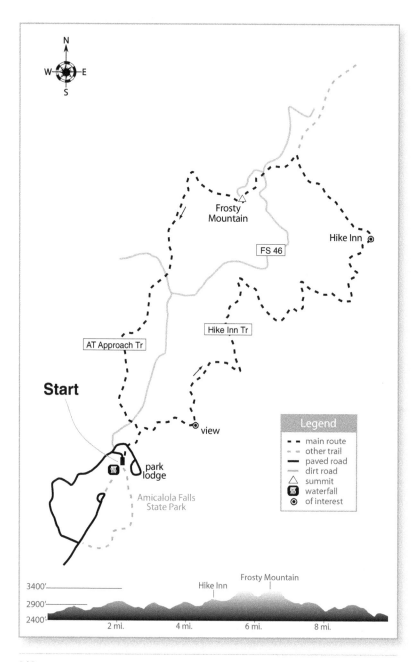

🥾 Wildcat Creek Trail

Hike Distance	8 miles
Type of Hike	Out & Back
Difficulty	Moderate
Hiking Time	3/4 Day
Start Elevation	1,486 ft
Total Ascent	600 ft
Land Manager	GA DNR
Fee	Yes*

* Georgia Outdoor Recreation Pass or GA hunting/fishing license required; not available at trailhead. Purchase online at georgiawildlife.com.

The highest falls you'll see on Fall Creek is 80 feet.

T he Georgia Department of Natural Resources manages several tracts of land as the Dawson Forest. Primarily the tracts are used by hunters and fishermen. More recently other forest users, including hikers, have been finding these lands as well. On the Wildcat Tract just southwest of Amicalola Falls State Park, a volunteer group called Mountain Stewards has marked and signed a number of trails. The best of these follows Wildcat Creek and leads to a number of waterfalls on Fall Creek. You'll walk to three of those falls on this hike.

It's comforting to hike along a stream, and you'll do that from the start as the trail sticks close to the shores of Wildcat Creek and Fall Creek the entire way. The first real landmark is a footbridge. Farther along it gets exciting. You have to ford the creek with the help of hand cables. Not too far beyond that is a side trail to the base of the first waterfall. Back on the main trail you'll pass another waterfall that takes a little bushwhacking to actually see, and finally at the far end of the hike you'll come to the highest waterfall yet. The good news is, it's right beside the trail.

Getting to the Trailhead

From Amicalola Falls State Park, travel west on GA 52 for 1.5 miles and bear left on GA 183. Drive 1.2 miles and turn right on GA 136. Continue 1.6 miles and turn left on Steve Tate Highway. Go 2.2 miles and turn right on Wildcat Campground Road. Drive 1.0 mile all the way to the back of the campground to the trailhead.

GPS Coordinates
N 34° 29.74' W 84° 16.93'

★=Start

Amicalola Falls State Park

Dahlonega

Steve Tate Hwy

Dawsonville

Hiking Directions

Begin Walk out of the back of the campground on Wildcat Creek Trail, following the creek.

Mile 1.7 You'll pass a footbridge here. Stay to the right on Wildcat Creek Trail.

Mile 2.1 Ford Wildcat Creek. There are cables here to help you. Just a little way after crossing the creek, the trail forks. Take the right fork. This is the spur trail

to the fourth falls on Fall Creek, a tributary of Wildcat Creek. You'll pass a beaver pond on the way.

Mile 2.4 The spur trail brings you to the fourth falls on Fall Creek, a 60-footer. Return to Wildcat Creek Trail and turn right on Fall Creek Trail.

Mile 3.1 You'll likely walk well beyond the place where you need to turn to bushwhack up to view the third falls, and realize it only when you hear the falls crashing loudly below the trail on the right. If you really want to see it, make a mental note of where you are and visit it on your return.

Mile 4.0 A short spur trail with a sign turns off to the left to take you to the base of the second falls on Fall Creek. This is the highest of the bunch at 80 feet, with a pool at the bottom. Return to the trailhead the way you came. If you missed the third falls on the way in, you can check it out on the return—here's how: When you again hear the third falls crashing on your left, continue down the hill to where the trail levels out. Now turn left and bushwhack back upstream alongside the creek. The going is not difficult; work your way around the rhododendron thickets, and in about 100 yards you'll find yourself at the bottom of a 50-foot waterfall. After viewing the falls, return to Wildcat Creek Trail and continue on downstream.

Mile 8.0 Finish.

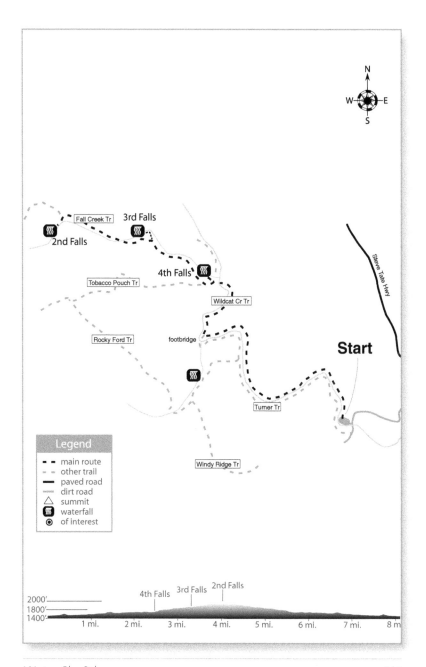

Fall Creek Tr

3rd Falls

2nd Falls

4th Falls

Tobacco Pouch Tr

Wildcat Cr Tr

Rocky Ford Tr

footbridge

Start

Steve Tate Hwy

Turner Tr

Windy Ridge Tr

Legend
- - main route
- - other trail
— paved road
= dirt road
△ summit
▦ waterfall
◉ of interest

2000'
1800'
1400'

4th Falls   3rd Falls   2nd Falls

1 mi.   2 mi.   3 mi.   4 mi.   5 mi.   6 mi.   7 mi.   8 m

Cohutta Mountains

The Cohuttas viewed from Fort Mountain

🚶 Jacks River Falls

Hike Distance	8.9 miles
Type of Hike	Out & Back
Difficulty	Moderate
Hiking Time	All Day
Start Elevation	1,564 ft
Total Ascent	1,069 ft
Land Manager	USFS
Fee	None

You'll enter the Cohutta Wilderness from Tennessee's Cherokee National Forest.

Jacks River Falls is probably the best-known destination in the entire Cohutta Wilderness, and this hike uses the quickest and most popular route to get there. The falls itself is huge, gorgeous, and remote—no wonder it's so popular. Its thundering noise alone commands attention.

You'll actually begin this hike in Tennessee, and getting to the trailhead requires a long drive in on a winding forest road. Once on the trail, you'll soon find yourself back in Georgia as you walk down the old roadbed known as Beech Bottom Trail. As the name implies, the trail leads to Beech Bottom, a relatively flat area of beech trees located upstream of the Jacks River Falls. It used to be a popular campsite, but due to overuse, camping is now forbidden anywhere near the falls. From Beech Bottom it's just a hop, skip, and a jump down to the waterfall. With a little scrambling on the rocks, you can make it down to the large plungepool below. On a hot day, it's an ideal spot for a swim.

Getting to the Trailhead

From Cisco on US 411, take Old GA 2 to the Jacks River Bridge, 8.7 miles. Bear right onto FS 221, go 1.2 miles and turn right on FS 62. Continue another 5.7 miles, and the Beech Bottom trailhead will be on the left.

GPS Coordinates
N 34° 59.43′ W 84° 35.30′

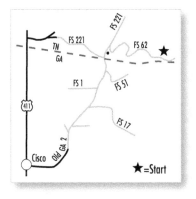

Hiking Directions

Begin Cross the road to the signboard and continue past it and onto the trail.

Mile 3.4 Bottom out at Beech Bottom. It's a little confusing here because the creek has washed out the trail. You'll need to ford the creek and continue on the trail on the other side.

Mile 4.0 After going up and over a small hill you'll come to the Jacks River. Turn right on Jacks River Trail and walk downstream.

Mile 4.5 Ford Beech Creek

again onto the bare rock on the other side. You should hear the roar of the falls just below. Continue down the right side of the river to the falls. It's a great place to spend some time on the rocks or in the water below the falls. When you're ready for the return hike, work your way back to mile 4.5. Cross Beech Creek and turn left, then follow the creek back to mile 3.4, fording the stream in several places. This is different from the way you came in along Jacks River. When you arrive back at Beech Bottom, turn left on Beech Bottom Trail and return the way you came.

Mile 8.9 Finish.

Jacks River Falls thunders over two dros into a large plungepool.

Jacks River Falls Trail Map

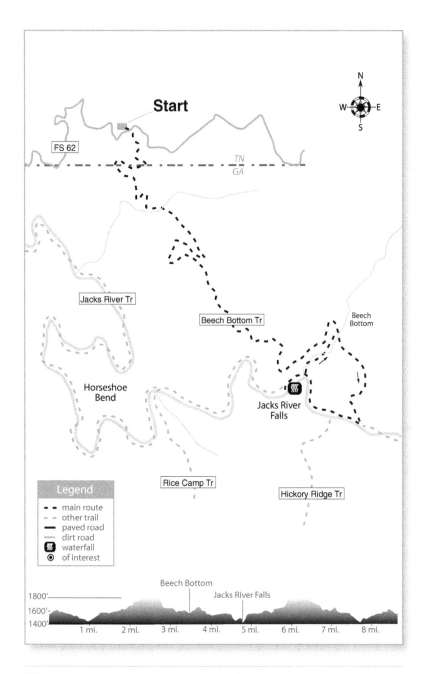

Start

FS 62

TN
GA

Jacks River Tr

Beech Bottom Tr

Beech
Bottom

Horseshoe
Bend

Jacks River
Falls

Rice Camp Tr

Hickory Ridge Tr

Legend
- main route
- other trail
- paved road
- dirt road
- waterfall
- of interest

Beech Bottom

Jacks River Falls

1800'
1600'
1400'
1 mi. 2 mi. 3 mi. 4 mi. 5 mi. 6 mi. 7 mi. 8 mi.

🥾 Rice Camp Loop

Hike Distance	11.6 miles
Type of Hike	Loop
Difficulty	Strenuous
Hiking Time	All Day
Start Elevation	1,777 ft
Total Ascent	2,826 ft
Land Manager	USFS
Fee	None

Signs in the Cohutta Wilderness are few and far between.

Plan to get to the trailhead early and stay out all day; this is a long and difficult day hike. That's just how things are if you connect trails to make a loop in the Cohutta Wilderness. Is it worth it? You bet. You'll walk across high ridges, ford rivers, and see remote waterfalls. That's a lot to see and do in a day.

This hike begins at the end of a long forest road, deep in the heart of the Cohutta Mountains. On the way to the trailhead you'll have to ford one stream twice in your vehicle, so high clearance is required. If the stream looks too high to cross, consider hiking elsewhere, because it indicates the Jacks River might also be running too high to ford on foot later in the day. Once on the trail you'll climb forever to get to the top of Hickory Ridge, where you'll walk a ways before dropping down to the Jacks River. Then it's downstream to Jacks River Falls, the ideal spot for lunch and a well-deserved break. From the falls, the route continues downstream to another ford before making a long return to the trailhead on Rice Camp Trail.

Getting to the Trail

From Cisco on US 411, take Old GA 2 to Cottonwood Patch Campground, 8.0 miles. Turn right here on FS 51 and drive another 4.8 miles to the end of the road and trailhead. *Caution:* Two big stream fords on FS 51.

GPS Coordinates
N 34° 57.02' W 84° 36.31'

★=Start

Hiking Directions

Begin From the trailhead, head uphill on East Cowpen Trail. The trail forks almost immediately. Continue on left fork.

Mile 2.7 After a long and sometimes steep climb, you'll finally gain the top of the ridge. Turn left onto Hickory Ridge Trail.

Mile 5.9 A steep downhill brings you to Jacks River. Cross to the other side (this can be a deep ford; scouting up or downstream may provide better options), and turn left on Jacks River Trail.

Mile 6.2 Ford Beech Creek;

Jacks River Falls is just below. You can view the upper falls by scrambling down to the rock slabs beside the plungepool. To reach the plungepool of the lower (and much taller) falls, follow the trail as it skirts the right side high above the falls. Access the bottom pool by any of several user-created goatpaths. The route continues down the right side of the river.

Mile 7.5 Ford Jacks River (use caution; this one is really slippery), and bear right where you'll cross a small stream. Continue downstream another 100 yards, and turn left on Rice Camp Trail.

Mile 10.5 Many stream crossings later and just off the trail to the right is the small Rice Camp Creek Falls. It sits just above a rocky bluff.

Mile 11.6 Finish.

The Jacks River Trail follows an old logging railroad bed.

Rice Camp Loop Trail Map

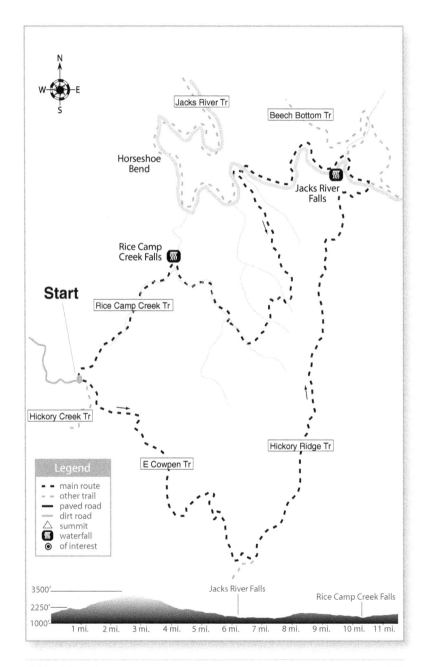

Jacks River Tr

Beech Bottom Tr

Horseshoe
Bend

Jacks River
Falls

Rice Camp
Creek Falls

Start

Rice Camp Creek Tr

Hickory Creek Tr

E Cowpen Tr

Hickory Ridge Tr

Legend
- - - main route
- - - other trail
— paved road
— dirt road
△ summit
🌊 waterfall
◉ of interest

3500'
2250'
1000'

Jacks River Falls

Rice Camp Creek Falls

1 mi. 2 mi. 3 mi. 4 mi. 5 mi. 6 mi. 7 mi. 8 mi. 9 mi. 10 mi. 11 mi.

🥾 Panther Creek Falls

Hike Distance	10.6 miles
Type of Hike	Out & Back
Difficulty	Strenuous
Hiking Time	All Day
Start Elevation	2,376 ft
Total Ascent	2,254 ft
Land Manager	USFS
Fee	None

Panther Creek Falls is right in the center of the Cohutta Wilderness Area.

Right smack dab in the middle of the Cohutta Wilderness Area you'll find Panther Creek Falls. If you've ever driven out to the edge of the Wilderness Area, you know it requires long miles on bumpy dirt roads. You can guess that getting to the middle of it is no easy feat. Of the numerous ways to reach the falls, this is the least difficult. Get an early start all the same.

On this route, you begin on the west boundary of the Cohutta Wilderness at the Hickory Creek Trailhead. From there, you'll drop down all the way to the upper portions of the Conasauga River where you'll find a stretch of flat country and a popular campsite that was once a farm. After walking along the shores of the river a short distance, you'll turn off onto the Panther Creek Trail, following Panther Creek upstream. This trail takes you first to the base and then to the top of the waterfall. It is not easy going; you don't really walk the trail as it rises beside the falls—you climb and rockhop up a steep jumble of boulders where trail blazes are few and far between.

Getting to the Trailhead

From Crandall on US 411, go east on Grassy Street. Cross the railroad tracks and turn right on Crandall Ellijay Road, then immediately left onto Mill Creek Road. This road becomes FS 630 when you enter the national forest. Continue another 6.2 miles past Hickey Gap Campground at the junction of FS 17. Stay on FS 630 another 0.3 mile to the trailhead.

GPS Coordinates
N 34° 54.11' W 84° 38.60'

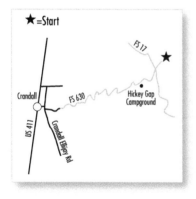

Hiking Directions

Begin From the trailhead, hike downhill on Hickory Creek Trail.

Mile 1.7 Junction of Conasauga River and Conasauga River Trail. Bear right along the river on Hickory Creek Trail/Conasauga River Trail.

Mile 3.0 Enter a large open area. Hickory Creek Trail fords the river here. Don't cross, but turn right and in a short distance Tearbritches Trail will exit uphill to the right. Don't take it, either. Continue across a small stream, follow the trail up a short hill, and then return to the river.

Mile 3.9 Turn left and ford the river onto Panther Creek Trail. Begin to ascend along Panther Creek.

Mile 5.0 Cross Panther Creek below a cascade. From here to the top of the falls, the trail climbs steeply through a boulder garden. Keep your eye peeled for trail blazes, and remember—as long as the creek is to your right and you are climbing, that's good. Near the top, you'll see that the trail climbs through a cleft in the cliff that forms the falls. Blazes guide the way, but if you miss them, look for a break in the cliff a few hundred feet to the left of the falls.

Mile 5.3 Finally—the top! Expect a great view here and a nice place for a break right at the lip of the falls. Return the way you came, taking care going down through the boulder field.

Mile 10.6 Finish.

Panther Creek Falls Trail Map

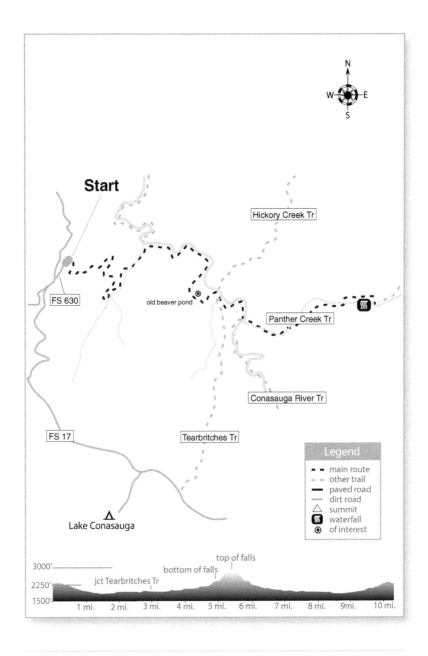

Start

Hickory Creek Tr

FS 630

old beaver pond

Panther Creek Tr

Conasauga River Tr

FS 17

Tearbritches Tr

Lake Conasauga

Legend
- ▪ ▪ main route
- - - other trail
- ▬ paved road
- --- dirt road
- △ summit
- 🌊 waterfall
- ◉ of interest

top of falls

bottom of falls

jct Tearbritches Tr

3000'

2250'

1500'

1 mi. 2 mi. 3 mi. 4 mi. 5 mi. 6 mi. 7 mi. 8 mi. 9mi. 10 mi.

⛰ Grassy Mountain Tower

Hike Distance	4.9 miles
Type of Hike	Combo
Difficulty	Moderate
Hiking Time	Half Day
Start Elevation	3,154 ft
Total Ascent	685 ft
Land Manager	USFS
Fee	None

You can climb to the first landing on the tower stairs for a 360-degree view.

Lookout towers are becoming scarce in the north Georgia mountains, so whenever you can find a trail heading up to one, take it—the tower will not last forever. This route takes you up to the top of Grassy Mountain, high in the Cohuttas and just across the Holly Creek valley from Fort Mountain. Walk a few steps up the tower, and the views open up in all directions. That's one highlight of this hike; the other is the Songbird Trail, which encircles a small beaver pond and was built with birders in mind.

Your hike begins at the Conasauga Lake Recreation Area, at the end of a long series of winding, dusty forest roads. From the lake you'll hike up to the tower first. The foot trail leads through an acid cove forest, then through tunnels of rhododendron, and finally past huge old hemlocks. Once at the tower, you can soak in the views before returning to the Songbird Trail. On the return you'll loop around a series of beaver ponds where you can easily spot gnawed-off trees, beaver dams, and maybe even a beaver at work. Walk quietly through this area, and keep an eye and an ear open for songbirds.

Getting to the Trailhead

From milepost 8 on GA 52 west of Ellijay, take Gates Chapel Road 5.4 miles. Continue onto FS 90 for another 1.7 miles and turn right on FS 68. Drive 7.2 miles and bear left toward Lake Conasauga. Continue to the trailhead parking just before the boat ramp.

GPS Coordinates
N 34° 51.60' W 84° 39.16'

Hiking Directions

Begin Walk down the trail to the dam and then onto the combined Tower/Songbird Trail.

Mile 0.5 Bear right as Songbird Trail exits left.

Mile 0.8 Songbird Trail enters from left. Turn right on Tower Trail.

Mile 1.7 Join FS 49. Continue on it to the tower.

Mile 2.1 Reach tower. After getting in your look, return to Tower/Songbird Trail.

Mile 3.5 Turn right on Songbird Trail.

Mile 3.8 Bear left as a trail enters from right.

Mile 4.2 Reach a boardwalk leading out into a beaver pond.

Mile 4.4 Turn right, back to the lake.

Mile 4.7 At the dam, turn right.

Mile 4.9 Finish.

A boardwalk leads into a beaver pond on the Songbird Trail.

Grassy Mountain Tower Trail Map

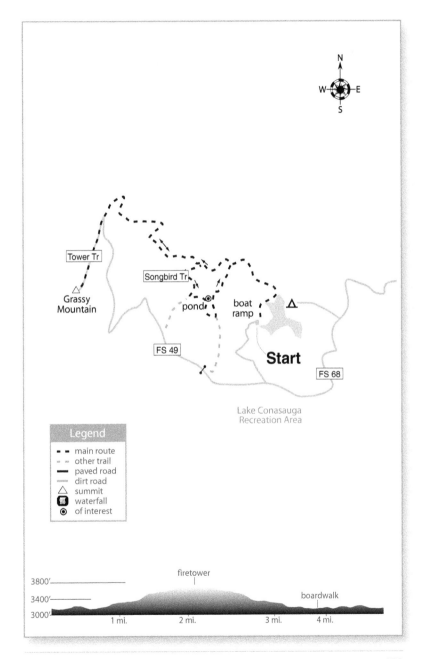

Tower Tr

Songbird Tr

Grassy
Mountain

pond

boat
ramp

FS 49

Start

FS 68

Lake Conasauga
Recreation Area

Legend
- - main route
- - - other trail
- ▬ paved road
- — dirt road
- △ summit
- 🌀 waterfall
- ◉ of interest

firetower

boardwalk

3800'
3400'
3000'

1 mi.　　2 mi.　　3 mi.　　4 mi.

⚎ Little Bald Mountain View

Hike Distance	1 mile
Type of Hike	Out & Back
Difficulty	Easier
Hiking Time	1 hour
Start Elevation	3,645 ft
Total Ascent	270 ft
Land Manager	USFS
Fee	None

The

This is one of those short hikes that you don't really want to make a special trip to do—but you won't want to pass it up if you find yourself in the neighborhood. Folks driving the forest road encircling the Cohutta Wilderness might want to use this as a leg stretcher. An extra option for ambitious summit baggers is to cross the road after walking out to the overlook and make the steep climb on Tearbritches Trail to the top of Bald Mountain. It adds one steep mile to the total distance and takes you to a 4,005-foot peak in the Cohutta Wilderness.

You'll start this hike from the trailhead for Tearbritches Trail and walk out across a large field known as the Little Bald campsite. On the far side of the opening you'll enter the woods on Emery Creek Trail. From here it's a short, slightly downhill walk out to the overlook—a rock outcrop area that has been cleared of trees. The view is fantastic.

Getting to the Trailhead

From milepost 8 on GA 52 west of Ellijay, take Gates Chapel Road 5.4 miles. Continue onto FS 90 for another 1.7 miles and turn right on FS 68. Drive 6.8 miles to the Tearbritches/Emery Creek trailhead.

GPS Coordinates
N 34° 51.67' W 84° 38.10'

Hiking Directions

Begin Walk up the old roadbed as it crosses the field through the Little Bald campsite.

Mile 0.1 At the end of the field, bear left onto the Emery Creek Trail.

Mile 0.5 Reach the rock outcrop overlook. You can clearly see Fort Mountain in the distance, along with other peaks. Retrace your steps from here to the trailhead.

Mile 1.0 Finish.

Benchmarks

This benchmark is located atop Coosa Bald.

Few mountains, if any, in the southeastern United States have not been surveyed by the U.S. Geological Survey. What can now be done with satellite imagery and global positioning systems was once done by humans on the ground. As you can see in the photo above, Coosa Bald was surveyed and marked in 1934. The people who did the survey walked up there with all their equipment, which you can bet was a lot heavier and bulkier than what we have today. Should you find yourself atop a high peak, poke around a bit. Chances are you'll find a benchmark like this one embedded in a rock.

Little Bald Mountain View Trail Map

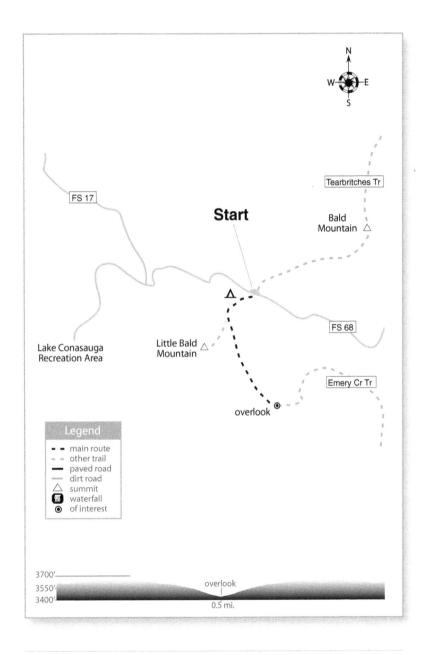

N
W — E
S

Tearbritches Tr

FS 17

Start

Bald
Mountain △

△

Lake Conasauga
Recreation Area

Little Bald △
Mountain

FS 68

Emery Cr Tr

overlook ◉

Legend
- ▪ ▪ main route
- ‑ ‑ other trail
- ▬ paved road
- — dirt road
- △ summit
- 🌀 waterfall
- ◉ of interest

3700'
3550'
3400'

overlook

0.5 mi.

⛰ Panther Bluff View

Hike Distance	8.6 miles
Type of Hike	Out & Back
Difficulty	Strenuous
Hiking Time	All Day
Start Elevation	3,507 ft
Total Ascent	1,930 ft
Land Manager	USFS
Fee	None

A hiker prepares lunch on the bluff at
the brink of Panther Creek Falls.

Hikers wanting to take in the view from the top of Panther Creek Falls
in the heart of the Cohutta Wilderness have several options for getting
there. This hike represents the top-down approach. It's the shortest way
in, but due to the steepness of the terrain, it's certainly not the easiest. The
route takes you to an area known as Panther Bluff; the bluff is what forms
the waterfall. You'll hike to the very brink of the falls, which offers the best
view in the Cohutta Wilderness.

Starting from the Three Forks trailhead, the trail leads you out along
the flanks of Cowpen Mountain, following the route of Old Highway
2. Nothing about this dirt path resembles a highway, but you can see
that it was once an old road. Soon you'll turn onto Panther Creek Trail,
which drops steeply through a high cove forest. You'll know you're getting close to Panther Bluff when you start noticing campsites beside the
creek. This is a popular place to camp, and it's no wonder with the falls
so close by. Your turnaround point is the lip of the falls. You'll want to
take a break and enjoy the view before the long uphill return.

Getting to the Trailhead

From milepost 8 on GA 52 west of Ellijay, take Gates Chapel Road 5.4 miles. Continue onto FS 90 for another 1.7 miles and turn right on FS 68. Drive 3.3 miles and turn right on FS 64, then go 4.3 miles to the East Cowpen Trailhead at Three Forks.

GPS Coordinates
N 34° 52.89' W 84° 33.94'

April this area is carpeted in trout lily.

Mile 4.3 Reach Panther Bluff. You can see the brink of the falls just ahead of you. Take care not to get too close to the edge; a slip would be deadly. After taking a break here, return up the mountain the way you came down.

Mile 8.6 Finish.

Hiking Directions

Begin Walk around the gate and onto East Cowpen Trail.

Mile 0.4 Rough Ridge Trail exits on the right. Stay on East Cowpen Trail.

Mile 2.3 Turn left onto Panther Creek Trail.

Mile 3.1 The trail begins to drop steeply here.

Mile 3.9 Cross Panther Creek to a beautiful campsite. In mid-

Signs in the wilderness area are weathered and worn.

Panther Bluff View Trail Map

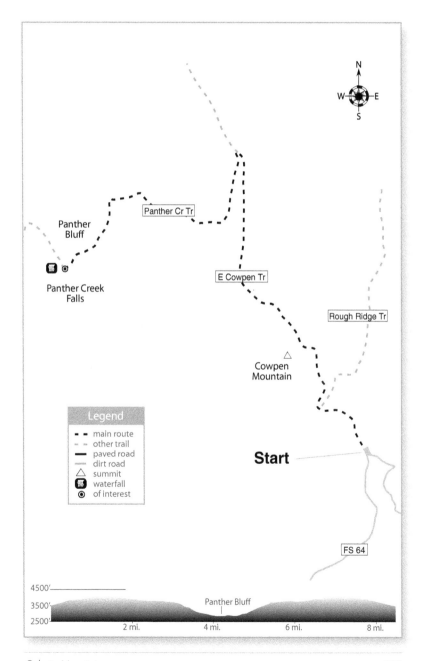

Legend
- ▪ ▪ main route
- ‑ ‑ other trail
- ▬ paved road
- ▬ dirt road
- △ summit
- 🌊 waterfall
- ◉ of interest

Panther Cr Tr

Panther Bluff

Panther Creek Falls

E Cowpen Tr

Rough Ridge Tr

△ Cowpen Mountain

Start

FS 64

4500'
3500'
2500'

Panther Bluff

2 mi.   4 mi.   6 mi.   8 mi.

Fowler Mountain View

Hike Distance	12.2 miles
Type of Hike	Out & Back
Difficulty	Strenuous
Hiking Time	All Day
Start Elevation	2,890 ft
Total Ascent	3,050 ft
Land Manager	USFS
Fee	None

A hiker rockhops through a stream under a
tangle of rhododendron.

The folks who laid out the Benton MacKaye Trail had quite a challenge linking together sections of public land for the trail to travel through. On this route, you'll hike through a remote section of national forest that connects the western Blue Ridge to the Cohutta Mountains. Your destination is the summit of Fowler Mountain, a lonesome knob that lies along the Tennessee Divide. This is a long and strenuous hike with steep-pitched climbs that will get your heart rate up. It's best completed during a season when no leaves are on the trees. Then the views, of which there are plenty, are much more open.

Not only does this hike take you through a remote area of forest, the trailhead itself is a long way from anywhere. You'll begin at Dyer Gap, where the Benton MacKaye Trail crosses FS 64 near the USFS Jacks River Fields campground. The trail immediately heads up to the summit of Flat Top Mountain where a firetower once stood. From here it's up and down all the way to the summit of Fowler Mountain, where the trail turns east and you turn around.

Getting to the Trailhead

From Blue Ridge, take GA 5 north for 3.7 miles, turn left on Old GA 2, and continue another 10.5 miles to Watson Gap. Turn left on FS 64 for 3.2 miles to Dyer Gap Cemetery, where the Benton MacKaye Trail crosses the road and FS 64A enters from the left.

GPS Coordinates
N 34° 52.11' W 84° 30.88'

Hiking Directions

Begin Walk up FS 64A following white diamond blazes.

Mile 0.3 Turn right off the dirt road onto a foot trail.

Mile 1.4 Top of Flat Top Mountain. Turn right past an old firetower site and continue on the trail.

Mile 2.9 Continue straight at the 4-way junction of forest roads.

Mile 4.6 Reach a saddle after the third hilltop. Off the trail to

the right here are several rock outcrops with good views to the south and west.

Mile 5.4 On either side of the trail notice large piles of rocks, which look as if they have been around for a long time. Why they are here is anyone's guess.

Mile 6.1 Reach the summit of Fowler Mountain. Here the trail makes an abrupt turn to the east (left). With no leaves on the trees, the views are good. When you're ready, turn around and head back to the trailhead the way you came.

Mile 12.2 Finish.

White diamonds blaze the Benton MacKaye Trail.

Fowler Mountain View Trail Map

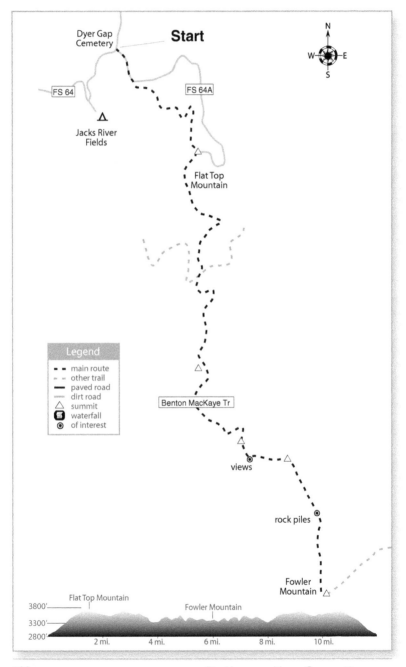

Dyer Gap Cemetery

Start

N
W E
S

FS 64

FS 64A

Jacks River Fields

Flat Top Mountain

Legend

- main route
- other trail
- paved road
- dirt road
- summit
- waterfall
- of interest

Benton MacKaye Tr

views

rock piles

Fowler Mountain

Flat Top Mountain

3800'

Fowler Mountain

3300'

2800'

2 mi.   4 mi.   6 mi.   8 mi.   10 mi.

DAY HIKING THE NORTH GEORGIA MOUNTAINS

🥾 Emery Creek Trail

Hike Distance	6.4 miles
Type of Hike	Out & Back
Difficulty	Moderate
Hiking Time	3/4 Day
Start Elevation	1,040 ft
Total Ascent	1,000 ft
Land Manager	USFS
Fee	None

The first falls you'll reach on Emery Creek is 60 feet high.

Wet feet? You bet. Hiking up to the waterfalls that adorn Emery Creek requires fording the stream eight times going up and eight more times coming down. You'll want to wear a pair of shoes you don't mind getting wet. Otherwise you'll drive yourself crazy getting them off and on, trying to find spots to rockhop across, or getting wet all over if you fall in while trying to tiptoe across slippery river stones barefoot. Just step in with your shoes on. The wet crossings are definitely worth the effort, as you'll see five pretty waterfalls.

The hike begins just upstream of the USFS Holly Creek Campground east of Chatsworth on FS 18. The area around the trailhead is a popular summer spot, with sun worshippers and swimmers hanging out on the rocks and in the small pools of Holly Creek. Soon you'll leave all those folks behind as you trek up to the falls on Emery Creek. A spur trail leads up to the first two. The third, fourth, and fifth falls are in a group farther upstream. These you'll find just off the shoulder of the trail; they require a little scrambling down the bank to see from the best vantage point.

Getting to the Trailhead

Head west from Ellijay on GA 52. Just before the climb up Fort Mountain and beyond milepost 12, turn right on Conasauga Road. Go 1.2 miles to where the pavement ends. Continue straight onto FS 18 for another 5.0 miles to the trailhead parking lot on the right.

GPS Coordinates
N 34° 48.74′ W 84° 39.13′

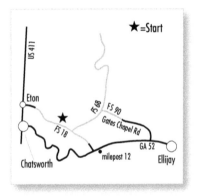

Hiking Directions

Begin Head out of the back of the parking lot onto Emery Creek Trail which follows an old rocky roadbed.

Mile 0.3 Confluence of Emery and Holly Creek. Ford Holly and then Emery to continue.

Mile 1.3 The trail turns right onto a seeded roadbed.

Mile 1.4 Turn left off roadbed back onto trail. Do not ford the creek here.

Mile 2.2 Turn left onto a spur trail signed "To Emery Creek Falls."

Mile 2.3 Base of the first falls, a 60-footer with a nice pool at the bottom. There is a second falls above this one. After viewing, return to the main trail and turn left up the mountain.

Mile 3.2 Arrive at the third, fourth, and fifth falls, with the middle of these the highest at 40 feet. This is a good place to turn around.

Mile 6.4 Finish.

You'll see these remains of an old motor vehicle before you reach the first falls.

Emery Creek Trail Map

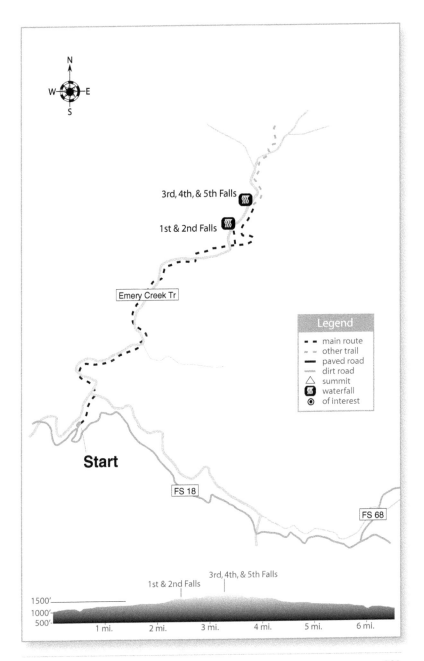

3rd, 4th, & 5th Falls

1st & 2nd Falls

Emery Creek Tr

Legend
- - - main route
- - - other trail
─── paved road
─── dirt road
△ summit
▨ waterfall
◉ of interest

Start

FS 18

FS 68

1st & 2nd Falls

3rd, 4th, & 5th Falls

1500'
1000'
500'

1 mi. 2 mi. 3 mi. 4 mi. 5 mi. 6 mi.

🥾 Stone Tower Loop

Hike Distance	2 miles
Type of Hike	Loop
Difficulty	Easier
Hiking Time	2 hours
Start Elevation	2,634 ft
Total Ascent	600 ft
Land Manager	State Park
Fee	$5

The stone lookout tower atop Fort Mountain is in need of repairs.

Mystery surrounds the top of Fort Mountain. High on this prominent peak is an ancient stone wall of unknown origin. Speculation abounds as to how it was created—involving everything from moon-eyed extraterrestrials to Hernando DeSoto. We'll probably never know for sure, but it makes for interesting conversation. This hike takes in a lot in a short distance—an observation platform looking out over the Great Valley, the precipitous North Face Trail, the old stone tower, and finally the ancient wall itself.

You'll begin from the Stone Tower Trailhead and walk up and over a hump before descending a set of steps leading to a wooden observation platform. Here you look west over the great valley toward Lookout Mountain and north into Tennessee. Then it's back up the steps and out onto the north face of Fort Mountain, where you'll circle around and walk up to the stone tower. From there you'll hike down along the famous wall before circling back to the trailhead.

Getting to the Trailhead

Fort Mountain State Park is located on GA 52 between Chatsworth and Ellijay. This route starts at the Stone Tower Trailhead parking lot.

GPS Coordinates
N 34° 46.70' W 84° 42.53'

Hiking Directions

Begin Walk up to the head of the parking lot and go immediately left on the yellow-blazed West Overlook Trail.

Mile 0.3 Stone Wall Trail enters from the right. Stay straight and then at the split, turn left on the red-blazed trail leading down the steps to the overlook.

Mile 0.4 Reach the overlook. From here, return to the trails junction and turn left onto North Face Trail, which has yellow blazes.

Mile 0.9 Look sharp for the steep, red-blazed Stone Tower Trail heading uphill to the right. Take it up past the junction with Stone Wall Trail to the tower.

Mile 1.1 Reach the stone tower and northern summit of Fort Mountain. From here, turn left on Stone Tower Trail.

Mile 1.2 At the ancient stone wall, turn left on blue-blazed Stone Wall Trail and walk along the wall.

Mile 1.4 Turn right on red-blazed Stone Tower Trail and then right again on yellow-blazed North Face Trail. You'll stay on this trail all the way back to the trailhead.

Mile 2.0 Finish.

To the north, rock outcrops along North Face Trail offer views of Grassy Mountain and beyond.

Stone Tower Loop Trail Map

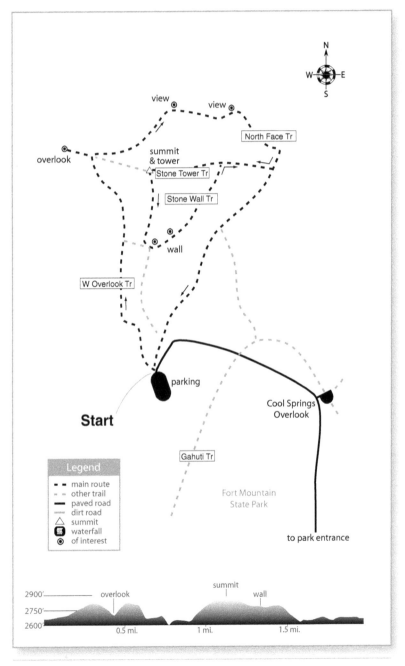

DAY HIKING THE NORTH GEORGIA MOUNTAINS

🚶🚶 Cool Springs Loop

Hike Distance	5.2 miles
Type of Hike	Loop
Difficulty	Moderate
Hiking Time	Half Day
Start Elevation	2,583 ft
Total Ascent	1,554 ft
Land Manager	State Park
Fee	$5

You'll pass a number of small waterfalls on the Cool Springs Loop.

The folks who run Fort Mountain State Park have done a good job with their trail system. Encircling the top portion of the mountain is a long back-country trail meant for overnight hiking. One step down the mountain is another long multi-use trail intended for mountain bikers, horseback riders, and hikers alike. On this hike, you'll connect two portions of each of these trails to form a loop underneath the Cool Springs Overlook. You'll pass several small waterfalls and a backcountry campsite and make a steep, switchbacking ascent to the end.

The loop begins at the Cool Springs Overlook. You can walk out and enjoy the view before and after your hike. From the trailhead, you'll first follow Gahuti Backcountry Trail as it heads north along the east face of the mountain. Before long it will drop you down to a backcountry campsite, and beyond there you'll turn onto East-West Trail #301. This takes you down to several waterfalls where the creek tumbles over green, moss-covered rocks that look like a staircase. From the creek, a steep climb brings you back to the overlook.

Getting to the Trailhead

Fort Mountain State Park is located on GA 52 between Chatsworth and Ellijay. This route starts at the Cool Springs Overlook parking lot. Be sure to stop at the park office to pick up a hiking permit.

GPS Coordinates
N 34° 46.73' W 84° 42.32'

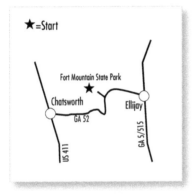

Hiking Directions

Begin Walk east on the Gahuti Trail, away from the overlook.

Mile 1.5 Cross the small stream and at campsite #1, turn left.

Mile 1.6 Cross the bridge and turn left onto East-West Trail #301.

Mile 2.4 After passing several small feeder stream falls you'll again reach Mill Creek. There is a 20-foot broken rock jumble falls here as well. The best view is from the trail.

Mile 2.8 Sluices and cascades along this stretch are more easily heard than seen. Look for a 20-foot-high stairstep waterfall that drops over a 50-foot distance.

Mile 2.9 Switchbacks lead down past a second stairstep falls which drops another 60 feet over a series of sluices and mossy rock tiers—very impressive.

Mile 3.3 Turn left at the #5 checkpoint and head steeply uphill.

Mile 3.7 Turn left off the forest road to stay on trail #301.

Mile 4.3 A series of steep, rocky switchbacks brings you to checkpoint #4. Turn left on trail #302.

Mile 5.0 Turn left on Gahuti Trail.

Mile 5.1 Cool Springs Observation Platform. Enjoy the view.

Mile 5.2 Finish.

From Cool Springs Overlook you look northeast toward the Cohutta Wilderness.

Cool Springs Loop Trail Map

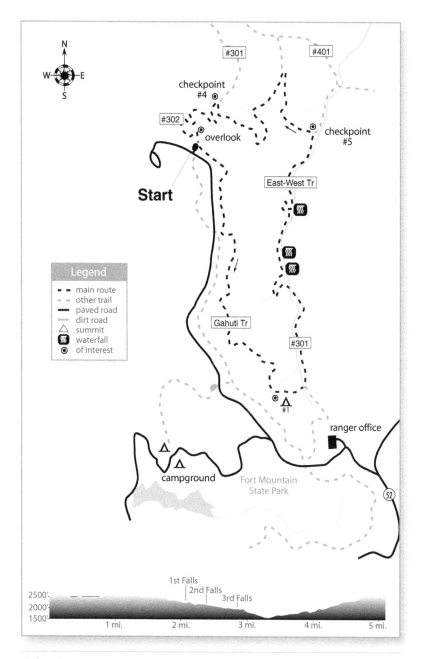

🚶‍♂️ West Face Loop

Hike Distance	5.7 miles
Type of Hike	Loop
Difficulty	Moderate
Hiking Time	Half Day
Start Elevation	2,583 ft
Total Ascent	1,174 ft
Land Manager	State Park
Fee	$5

Be sure to check out the view from Cool Springs Overlook before you start the hike.

While the Cool Springs Loop on the previous pages describes a loop route along the Gahuti Backcountry Trail at Fort Mountain State Park, the West Face Loop describes a circuit along another portion of the trail. On this one, you'll hike out along the west rim of the mountain where rock outcrop views look out over the Great Valley towards Chatsworth and Dalton, all the way to Lookout Mountain below Chattanooga, Tennessee. For the most part you'll stay on top of the mountain, which means the hill climbs are less fierce.

You'll begin this hike at the Cool Springs Overlook parking area and begin by walking north on the Gahuti Trail as it snakes under the summit of Fort Mountain. Once out on the west rim, you'll pass a backcountry campsite and then a couple of rock outcrop view spots. At one point you can hear a waterfall crashing below. At the far end of the route you'll turn onto Big Rock Nature Trail and climb past a stairstep waterfall. From the lake you'll walk up to the campground and then return via bike trail #302.

Getting to the Trailhead

Fort Mountain State Park is located on GA 52 between Chatsworth and Ellijay. This route starts at the Cool Springs Overlook parking lot. Be sure to stop at the park office to pick up a hiking permit.

GPS Coordinates
N 34° 46.73' W 84° 42.32'

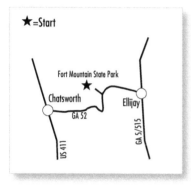

Hiking Directions

Begin Walk north on the Gahuti Trail.

Mile 0.1 Cross bike trail #302.

Mile 0.2 A connector trail exits right here. Stay to the left.

Mile 0.3 Cross road.

Mile 1.0 Reach first rock outcrop view.

Mile 2.0 Campers Loop Trail enters from the left.

Mile 2.2 Bear right and cross footbridge just after Campers Loop Trail exits to the left.

Mile 2.5 Cross Goldmine Creek and turn right to join Big Rock

Nature Trail. You'll pass alongside the upper falls on Goldmine Creek.

Mile 2.7 Reach another footbridge. Do not cross this one, but turn left off the Gahuti Trail and stay on Big Rock Nature Trail.

Mile 2.9 Reach trailhead for Big Rock Nature Trail. Turn left and walk across the dam on the road and continue up to the campground.

Mile 3.6 Turn left onto bike trail #301 at entrance to campground loop.

Mile 4.4 Reach the bicycle-use parking area. Turn left on bike trail #302.

Mile 5.1 Cross road.

Mile 5.7 Finish.

You'll pass Fort Mountain Lake about halfway around the loop.

West Face Loop Trail Map

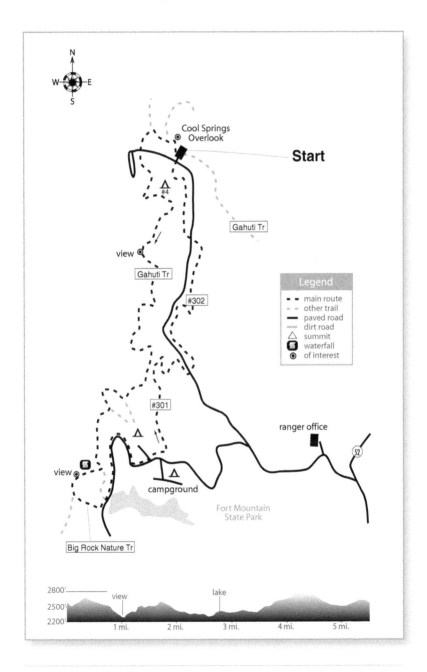

Cool Springs Overlook

Start

#4

Gahuti Tr

view

Gahuti Tr

#302

Legend

- main route
- other trail
- paved road
- dirt road
- △ summit
- 🌊 waterfall
- ◉ of interest

#301

ranger office

52

view

campground

Fort Mountain
State Park

Big Rock Nature Tr

2800'
view
2500'
2200'

lake

1 mi.   2 mi.   3 mi.   4 mi.   5 mi.

Just Where Is North Georgia, Anyhow?

Some say north Georgia is in the Southern Appalachian Mountains. Others say it's in the Blue Ridge. Both are correct, but it's complicated. North Georgia marks the southern terminus of the Blue Ridge Province, which is a part of the greater Appalachian Mountain chain.

Appalachian is an interesting word. It was given to us by the Spanish explorers when they first arrived in what is now Florida. There they found a Native American tribe called the Appalachee, and when the Spaniards marched northward, they named the first mountains they came to the Appalachians. Even though no Appalachees ever lived there, the name stuck.

The Appalachians begin as mere foothills in Alabama and run northward up the eastern seaboard to finally end in Newfoundland. The Appalachian Trail travels almost the full length of the Appalachian chain. Most of north Georgia is part of the southern Appalachians.

The Blue Ridge Province is a geologic area that stretches from south-central Pennsylvania to north Georgia and includes the highest peaks west of the Mississippi, with North Carolina's Mt. Mitchell the highest at 6,684 feet. Fort Mountain and the Cohuttas mark the far western edge of the Province.

Are all the mountains in north Georgia part of the same two chains? They are not. Pigeon Mountain and Lookout Mountain in the northwest are part of the Cumberland Plateau. And Kennesaw Mountain, nearer Atlanta, is part of the Appalachians but not the Blue Ridge.

Northwest Georgia

CLOUDLAND CANYON FROM ATOP LOOKOUT MOUNTAIN

🚶 West Rim Loop

Hike Distance	5 miles
Type of Hike	Loop
Difficulty	Moderate
Hiking Time	Half Day
Start Elevation	1,800 ft
Total Ascent	1,230 ft
Land Manager	State Park
Fee	$5

A series of overlooks connected by a foot trail surrounds the west rim of Cloudland Canyon.

Cloudland Canyon is one of the marvels of Northwest Georgia. Here in the Ridge and Valley Region, Lookout Mountain extends like a finger down into Georgia. This mountain, part of the Cumberland Plateau, is altogether different from those found in the Blue Ridge Province to the east. Flat on top with steep sides, these plateaus are broken up by canyons and gulches. Cloudland Canyon cuts a wide swath like a gaping mouth, and on this hike you'll walk around its west rim, hopping from overlook to overlook.

The route begins at the canyon overlook day-use parking and picnic area in Cloudland Canyon State Park. First you'll need to walk down, cross Sittons Creek, then hike back up to the west rim. This is the steepest climbing you'll do. Once on the west rim, the trail skirts the edge of sheer cliffs for much of its length. You'll visit eight different overlooks, all well defined with attractive fencing to keep folks from falling into the abyss. The views are spectacular.

Getting to the Trailhead

Cloudland Canyon State Park is located just west of the intersection of GA 136 and GA 189 atop Lookout Mountain, south of Chattanooga, TN.

GPS Coordinates
N 34° 50.01' W 85° 28.84'

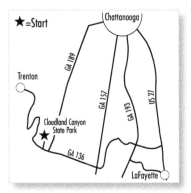

Hiking Directions

Begin Walk from the day-use parking area out to the east rim and turn left along the trail.

Mile 0.2 Follow the steps down, turning left at the West Rim Trail sign. You'll go down from here to cross Sittons Creek.

Mile 0.7 You're on the west side now. Turn right at the trail split, following the yellow blazes.

Mile 1.0 This is your first view from atop a large boulder. Continue to follow the yellow-blazed trail as it works its way around the rim.

Mile 1.3 A footbridge marks the

beginning of the loop. Turn right across the bridge to walk the loop counterclockwise.

Mile 2.8 Turn left here to stay on the loop. A right turn takes you to another parking area.

Mile 3.6 Reach the footbridge which marks the end of loop. Continue straight to retrace your steps back down, cross Sitton's Creek, and climb to the trailhead.

Mile 5.0 Finish.

A hiker surveys Cloudland Canyon from an overlook on its west rim.

West Rim Loop Trail Map

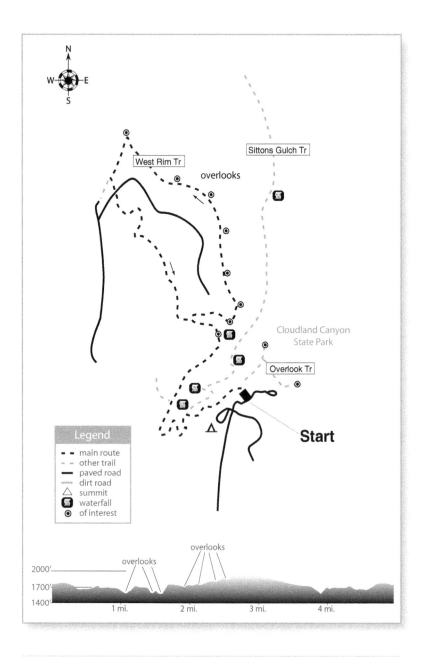

N
W–E
S

West Rim Tr

Sittons Gulch Tr

overlooks

Cloudland Canyon
State Park

Overlook Tr

Start

Legend
- - main route
- - other trail
— paved road
⚏ dirt road
△ summit
▦ waterfall
◉ of interest

overlooks

overlooks

2000'
1700'
1400'

1 mi.   2 mi.   3 mi.   4 mi.

🥾 Sittons Gulch Trail

Hike Distance	5.4 miles
Type of Hike	Out & Back
Difficulty	Moderate
Hiking Time	Half Day
Start Elevation	1,800 ft
Total Ascent	1,476 ft
Land Manager	State Park
Fee	$5

The second falls in Sittons Gulch
plunges straight off the cliff 100 feet.

When there are waterfalls around, it's nearly impossible not to want to visit them. At Cloudland Canyon State Park there are quite a few. The two most famous—in part because they are the most accessible—are the first and second falls on Sittons Creek in Sittons Gulch. All it takes to get to them is hiking from the picnic area down 600 steps attached to the side of the canyon. Sounds easy enough, but realize you have to come back up those same steps. Still, a lot of people make the trip. Not so many hike down the length of Sittons Gulch itself, where you'll find a number of smaller waterfalls, along with an excellent trail beside the creek.

This hike starts from the day-use area at Cloudland Canyon and quickly descends into Sittons Gulch. Once down on the canyon floor the trail crosses a suspension bridge, then follows Sittons Creek out to the mouth of the canyon. Here you'll make a small loop around a wildflower-rich bottom before returning to the trailhead the way you came. Along the creek look for small waterfalls, shoals, rapids, and swimming holes.

Getting to the Trailhead

Cloudland Canyon State Park is located just west of the intersection of GA 136 and GA 189 atop Lookout Mountain, south of Chattanooga, TN.

GPS Coordinates
N 34° 50.01' W 85° 28.84'

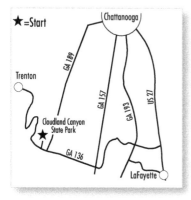

Hiking Directions

Begin From the day-use area, walk to the canyon rim and follow signs leading to the falls.

Mile 0.2 Bottom of first tier of steps. Turn right at the sign pointing to the falls.

Mile 0.3 Many steps later, turn left to first falls.

Mile 0.5 First falls. Return to the last junction and follow the trail/steps to second falls.

Mile 0.8 Reach bottom of steps. Turn left to second falls.

Mile 0.9 Second falls. Return to the last junction and follow signs onto Sittons Gulch Trail.

Mile 1.0 Cross Sittons Creek on a high bridge.

Mile 1.2 Cross a low-flow stream. When water is present in this stream, you'll see West Rim Falls to your left. If you walk upstream a short distance, you'll see that the falls is very high (180 feet or so) and begins on the top of the western rim.

Mile 2.5 Between here and West Rim Falls you'll pass numerous small waterfalls and swimming holes on Sittons Gulch Creek. Turn left here to begin the end-loop portion of trail.

Mile 2.7 Turn right at trail junction. The trail coming in from the left here should have a wire strung across it.

Mile 2.9 Close the loop and return to the trailhead the way you came down.

Mile 5.4 Finish.

Sittons Gulch Trail snakes its way along Sittons Creek.

Sittons Gulch Trail Map

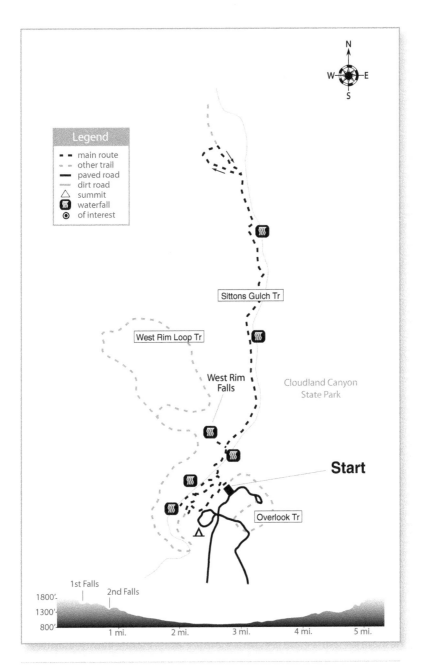

Legend
- - main route
- - other trail
— paved road
— dirt road
△ summit
🌊 waterfall
◉ of interest

N
W—E
S

Sittons Gulch Tr

West Rim Loop Tr

West Rim
Falls

Cloudland Canyon
State Park

Start

Overlook Tr

1st Falls
2nd Falls

1800'
1300'
800'
1 mi.   2 mi.   3 mi.   4 mi.   5 mi.

⛰ Zahnd Natural Area

Hike Distance	1.3 miles
Type of Hike	Out & Back
Difficulty	Easier
Hiking Time	2 hours
Start Elevation	2,086 ft
Total Ascent	100 ft
Land Manager	GA DNR
Fee	Yes*

* Georgia Outdoor Recreation Pass or GA hunting/fishing license required; not available at trailhead. Purchase online at georgiawildlife.com.

Strange-looking natural rock sculptures dominate the Zahnd Natural Area.

Located on Lookout Mountain and just across McLemore Cove from Pigeon Mountain, the Zahnd Natural Area is one of northwest Georgia's hidden gems. Here bizarre natural rock sculptures dominate the landscape. It's a boulderer's dreamscape. What's bouldering? To put it simply, it's freestyle (no ropes) rock climbing on relatively low boulders. Don't be surprised, then, if you see people with snug-fitting clothes spread-eagled on the rocks. They hone their skills here for more difficult cliff ascents.

The trail leading into the Zahnd Natural Area is unmarked but easy to navigate, at least out to the boulder area. Once among the boulders, various short trails lead off to different spots. The boulders themselves are roughly arranged along a low ridge, and the trail tends to enter the area on its northern end. Once you reach the boulders, just hang a right and walk along the base of the low ridge, giving yourself plenty of time to explore the unique formations. Eventually, you'll reach a spring issuing from a small cave—a good place to turn back.

Getting to the Trailhead

From Cloudland Canyon go 3.2 miles east on GA 136 and turn right on GA 157. Drive 10.1 miles to a pulloff on the left. The Zahnd Natural Area is just across the road and marked with a sign.

GPS Coordinates
N 34° 39.30' W 85° 28.17'

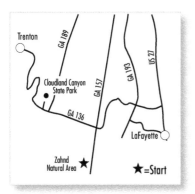

Hiking Directions

Begin First walk east, out the short trail on the same side of the road you're parked on, for a beautiful clifftop view of McLemore Cove and Pigeon Mountain.

Mile 0.1 Reach the clifftop view. Return to the trailhead and cross the road onto the trail into Zahnd Natural Area.

Mile 0.3 Enter an area of large boulders. Bear left and walk along the base of a low ridge. Side trails lead off to different boulders. Be sure to explore those, but always work your way

back to the main trail along the lower ridge.

Mile 0.7 Here you'll reach a good-sized spring coming out of a small cave under one of the boulders. The water is cool and refreshing, and this is a good place to turn around. You might want to take a slightly different path back to the trailhead.

Mile 1.3 Finish.

This interesting rock formation sits atop the cliff overlooking McLemore Cove.

Zahnd Natural Area Trail Map

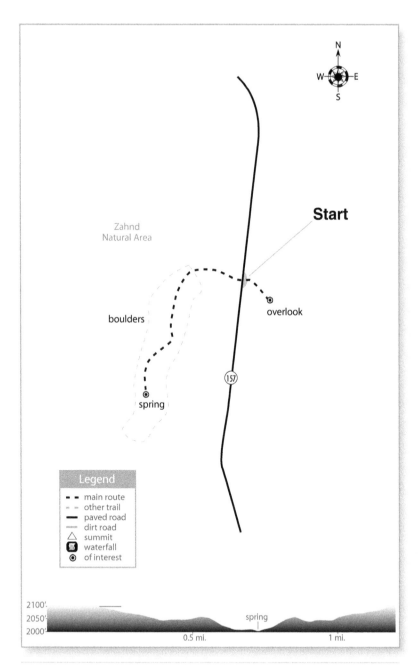

Zahnd
Natural Area

Start

overlook

boulders

157

spring

Legend
- ▬ ▬ main route
- ═ ═ other trail
- ▬ paved road
- ═ dirt road
- △ summit
- ▨ waterfall
- ◉ of interest

2100'
2050'
2000'

spring

0.5 mi.   1 mi.

🥾 High Point Loop

Hike Distance	9.9 miles
Type of Hike	Loop
Difficulty	Strenuous
Hiking Time	All Day
Start Elevation	909 ft
Total Ascent	1,948 ft
Land Manager	GA DNR
Fee	Yes*

* Georgia Outdoor Recreation Pass or GA hunting/fishing license required; not available at trailhead. Purchase online at georgiawildlife.com.

High Point offers several clifftop vantage points. This one overlooks McLemore Cove toward Lookout Mountain.

The high plateau of Pigeon Mountain attaches to Lookout Mountain like a thumb, with beautiful McLemore Cove in between. It's an interesting place with a wide range of users. Spelunkers know it as one of the largest underground cave networks in the Southeast. Climbers flock there for its cliffs and bouldering opportunities. Mountain bikers and horseback riders love its rugged trails. Hang-gliders soar on updrafts from its many launch sites. It's known by hunters for its abundant game. To hikers, it's a haven of solitude.

This route takes advantage of one of the few trails that climbs from the bottom of Pigeon Mountain to the top. You'll start in what is called the "Pocket," a cove with a pretty waterfall at its far end. From the get-go you'll be walking uphill, passing the waterfall within the first half-mile. The gradual four-mile ascent will get your legs burning and your blood pumping. Once at High Point, you can enjoy the view from several clifftop vantage points. The trail then loops back to the bottom of the Pocket, passing springs and small creeks along the way.

Getting to the Trailhead

Take GA 193 west of LaFayette to Davis Crossroads and turn left onto Hogjowl Road. Go 2.7 miles and turn left onto Pocket Road. It's 1.3 more miles to the trailhead. *Caution:* Shallow stream ford on Pocket Road.

GPS Coordinates
N 34° 42.76' W 85° 22.80'

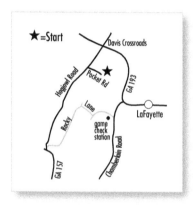

Hiking Directions

Begin From the trailhead parking area, go around the gate, and follow the old roadbed up the hill.

Mile 0.4 Turn right off the old road toward the falls.

Mile 0.5 Waterfall. After viewing, turn back to old road and go right on up above the falls.

Mile 0.7 Just past the top of the falls, turn right on South Pocket Trail. You'll follow blue blazes up the mountain.

Mile 3.3 A sometimes rocky climb brings you to the top of the mountain. Turn left along the brow onto what is now Pocket Loop Trail. West Brow Trail has entered from the right and now follows the same path as Pocket Loop.

Mile 4.1 As you travel along the western brow of Pigeon Mountain you'll have amazing clifftop views of McLemore Cove below and Lookout Mountain ahead. Here you reach the high point of the hike—the spot called High Point.

Mile 5.2 Turn left on gravel roadbed as Atwood Trail enters from the right.

Mile 6.3 Bear left to continue on Pocket Loop Trail. West Brow and then Cane Trail exit to the right.

Mile 9.1 The trail down the mountain is rocky and rigorous. In places it shows heavy wear from horse use. You'll bottom out in a large meadow.

Mile 9.4 Look for a pond on the right and a large spring on the left. The water from this spring forms much of Pocket Branch Falls just below.

Mile 9.5 Close the loop. Continue on down the old roadbed, past the waterfall, and back to the trailhead.

Mile 9.9 Finish.

High Point Loop Trail Map

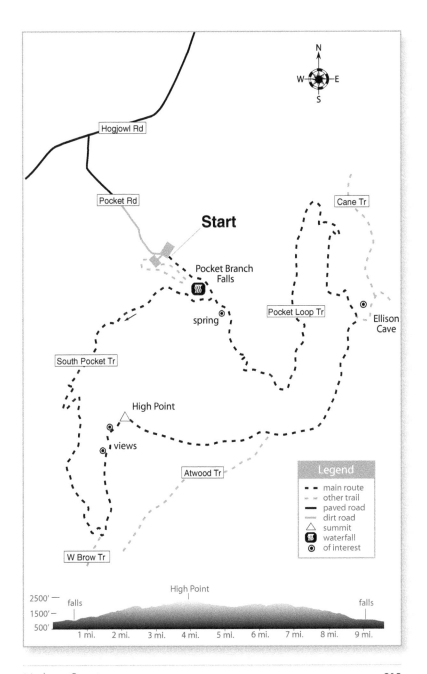

Hogjowl Rd

Pocket Rd

Cane Tr

Start

Pocket Branch Falls

Pocket Loop Tr

spring

Ellison Cave

South Pocket Tr

High Point

views

Atwood Tr

W Brow Tr

Legend

- - - main route
- - - other trail
— paved road
— dirt road
△ summit
▦ waterfall
◉ of interest

2500' —
1500' —
500' —

falls

High Point

falls

1 mi. 2 mi. 3 mi. 4 mi. 5 mi. 6 mi. 7 mi. 8 mi. 9 mi.

🥾 Rocktown Loop

Hike Distance	7.4 miles
Type of Hike	Loop
Difficulty	Moderate
Hiking Time	3/4 Day
Start Elevation	1,968 ft
Total Ascent	680 ft
Land Manager	GA DNR
Fee	Yes*

* Georgia Outdoor Recreation Pass or GA hunting/fishing license required; not available at trailhead. Purchase online at georgiawildlife.com.

Giant rocks sprout up like mushrooms in Rocktown atop Pigeon Mountain.

Rocktown is aptly named. No, it's not really a town with people living in it. It's an area on Pigeon Mountain with giant boulders scattered through the woods. These weathered rocks come in all kinds of shapes and it doesn't take much imagination to envision a colony of gnomes living among them. Some shoot up like wild skyscrapers, others blossom sideways like mushrooms with protected spaces underneath, looking like strange picnic pavilions. Still others have clefts down the middle, causing them to resemble warped toasters. Bouldering enthusiasts love it here, so don't be surprised to see them clambering over the rocks.

Most folks just drive out to the Rocktown trailhead and walk the mile-long trail to the boulders. On this hike, you'll take in a bit more. You'll first hike along the west brow of Pigeon Mountain, where there are good views to the west. From there you'll circle back past Allen Creek Falls and finally head into Rocktown itself. Start early so you will have plenty of time to explore once you arrive there.

Getting to the Trailhead

From LaFayette, take GA 193 north 2.8 miles and turn left on Chamberlain Road. Go 3.5 miles and turn right on Rocky Lane. Continue past the check station up the mountain all the way to Sawmill Camp camping site. *Caution:* Rocky Lane is steep and roughly paved with several tight switchbacks.

GPS Coordinates
N 34° 40.25' W 85° 23.26'

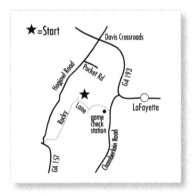

Hiking Directions

Begin From the campground walk back to, and then west on, Rocky Lane.

Mile 0.3 At the road junction, walk straight into the woods onto West Brow Trail.

Mile 1.2 There's a rock outcrop view from this high point on the trail.

Mile 2.5 Here you'll enter a cleared area that was once an old homesite. Continue out to Rocky Lane where you'll bear left on the road and then right after crossing the creek onto the trail.

Mile 3.6 Hood Trail turns off to the left here. Continue straight another 0.2 miles down to Allen Creek Falls and then return back here.

Mile 3.8 Just past the turn onto Atwood Trail you'll come to Allen Creek Falls. Turn back here to the Hood Trail.

Mile 4.2 Back at Hood Trail turn. Turn right on it.

Mile 5.1 Watch closely for a carsonite sign on the left side of the trail, bearing the mark 0.6. There is a faint cut-through trail here that connects to Rocktown. It's a bit of a leap of faith. Walk through the woods 100 feet, and you should run into the Rocktown Trail. You'll know it by its rose-colored blaze. Left goes into the far portion of Rocktown (where you may want to explore), but it's a right you'll need to take for the most direct route back to the trailhead.

Mile 6.2 Reach the trailhead for Rocktown Trail. Continue onto the dirt entrance road.

Mile 6.9 Turn left on Rocky Lane.

Mile 7.4 Turn right into the camping area to finish.

Rocktown Loop Trail Map

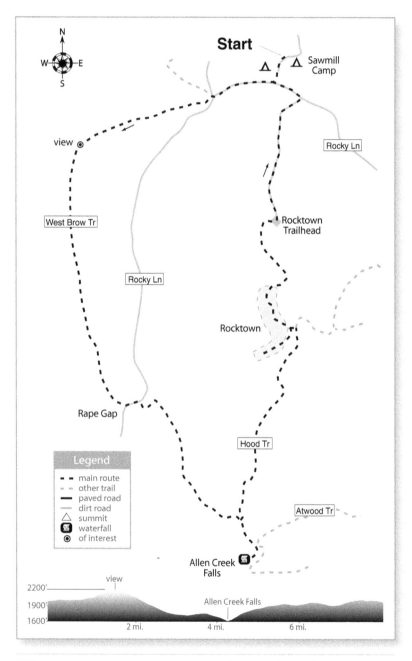

Start

△ △ Sawmill Camp

N
W   E
S

view ◉

Rocky Ln

West Brow Tr

Rocky Ln

Rocktown Trailhead

Rocktown

Rape Gap

Hood Tr

Legend
- - - main route
- - - other trail
—— paved road
===== dirt road
△ summit
♨ waterfall
◉ of interest

Atwood Tr

Allen Creek Falls ♨

view

2200'
1900'
1600'

Allen Creek Falls

2 mi.   4 mi.   6 mi.

🚶‍ Taylors Ridge Trail

Hike Distance	5 miles
Type of Hike	Out & Back
Difficulty	Easier
Hiking Time	Half Day
Start Elevation	1,444 ft
Total Ascent	600 ft
Land Manager	USFS
Fee	None

The hike starts at a gap on GA 136.
Look for the brown sign.

Just to the east of Lookout Mountain and Pigeon Mountain, the topography changes from a plateau to a ridge and valley landscape. Several long spines jut up the state running from south to north. The longest of these is Taylors Ridge, which stretches for 40 miles from just south of Summerville all the way to Ringgold. In contrast to its flat-topped neighbors, Taylors Ridge is more knifelike, with steep sides rising to a pointed top. From above, these ridges look like waves rippling across water.

Taylors Ridge Trail follows the top of the ridge for just a little over two miles. On this hike, you'll begin at the northern terminus on GA 136 near LaFayette and walk south. The route starts on an old roadbed and soon climbs to the top of the ridge on a short but steep foot trail. A foot trail it remains until ending abruptly at a junction with FS Route 635-A, the turnaround point. This hike is best done in cooler weather when the leaves are off the trees, and views into the surrounding valleys are ideal.

Getting to the Trailhead

From LaFayette, drive east 10.0 miles on GA 136, or from Villanow drive west 4.0 miles on GA 136. The trailhead pulloff is on the south side of the road.

GPS Coordinates

N 34° 41.32' W 85° 11.34'

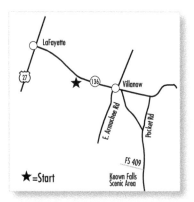

★=Start

Hiking Directions

Begin From the pulloff, walk around the gate onto the old road which is Taylors Ridge Trail.

Mile 0.5 Turn right off the old road onto the marked foot trail. Begin a steep climb to the top of the ridge.

Mile 2.5 You'll walk along the top of the ridge over numerous humplike summits and past several view spots before finally reaching a junction with FS 635-A. This is the turnaround point. Retrace your steps to the start.

Mile 5.0 Finish.

The Civil War in North Georgia

Natural walls like this made for great defense.

Most folks have heard of the Battle of Chickamauga or the Battle of Lookout Mountain. But how many have heard of the battle of Taylors Ridge? This Civil War battle was fought just south of Ringgold, not so far north of where you will be hiking on Taylors Ridge Trail. Here General Patrick Cleburne of the Confederate Army held off an attack by Union troops under the command of General Peter Osterhaus. At one point when the Confederates where out of ammunition, an all-out charge was ordered, and they chased the Yankees off the ridge with a hail of rocks and sticks. As you hike along the ridge you can see how easy it would be to defend the high ground here. There are plenty of boulders and trees to hide behind, and you have a commanding view of the valley below.

Taylors Ridge Trail Map

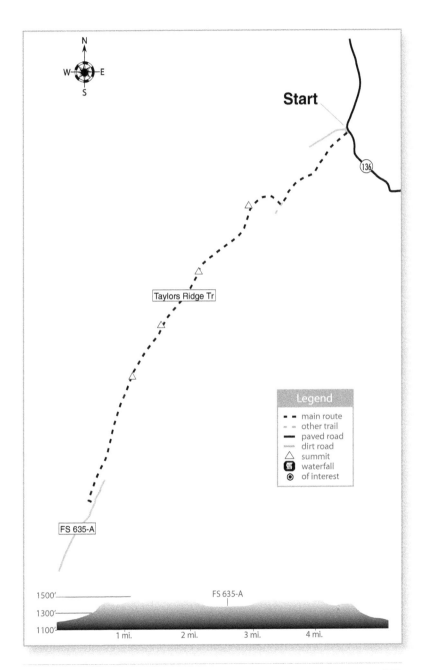

⛰ Johns Mountain Loop

Hike Distance	5 miles
Type of Hike	Loop
Difficulty	Moderate
Hiking Time	Half Day
Start Elevation	1,013 ft
Total Ascent	1,100 ft
Land Manager	USFS
Fee	None

The view from Johns Mountain looks out over the Armuchee Valley.

Neo matter how you slice it, you'll get in a good hike when you head out to Johns Mountain. Here, just north of the Pocket Recreation Area, a figure-eight loop trail ascends through the Keown Falls Scenic Area to the summit of Johns Mountain. Up on top you'll find an observation platform overlooking the rolling green farmland of Armuchee Valley.

Not only will you get a great view, you'll also see two waterfalls falling off a cliff only 0.3 mile apart. Be aware that these falls are fickle. They flow well only after periods of wet weather. Your best chances for a consistent flow are in winter and spring. Summers in northwest Georgia are typically hot and dry, which reduces these falls to a trickle, a drip, or nothing at all. No matter—the hike itself is a good one with views in all directions.

You'll begin at a nice picnic area, and the northernmost falls is the first highlight of the route. After climbing up and over Johns Mountain, you'll get to see the second one farther south.

Getting to the Trailhead

From I-75 just north of Calhoun, take GA 136 to Villanow. Turn left on Pocket Road and drive 6.0 miles. Turn right on gravel FS 409 and continue 0.7 mile to Keown Falls Scenic Area picnic area and trailhead.

GPS Coordinates
N 34° 36.80' W 85° 05.30'

Hiking Directions

Begin From the trailhead, hike through the A-frame trail entrance and onto the trail. You'll see both green (Keown Falls Trail) and white (Pinhoti Trail) blazes, as this section is shared by the two.

Mile 0.1 The trail splits here to begin the loop. Take the right fork, heading toward the overlook.

Mile 0.8 Just after a series of stone steps you'll reach Keown Falls North. Take a good look and then continue up the wooden steps to the viewing platform above the falls.

Mile 0.9 Turn right on Johns Mountain Trail.

Mile 1.7 Reach Johns Mountain Overlook. There is a parking area here which is at the end of a long and bumpy dirt road. Turn left to hike along the west brow of Johns Mountain.

Mile 3.9 Close the Johns Mountain Trail loop. Turn right down the steps to Keown Falls North. You've been here before. Go behind the falls and along the trail that follows the base of the cliff.

Mile 4.2 Reach Keown Falls South. Continue past it and down the mountain.

Mile 4.9 Close the loop for the bottom loop trail. Turn right.

Mile 5.0 Finish.

Medium flow at Keown Falls North.

Johns Mountain Loop Trail Map

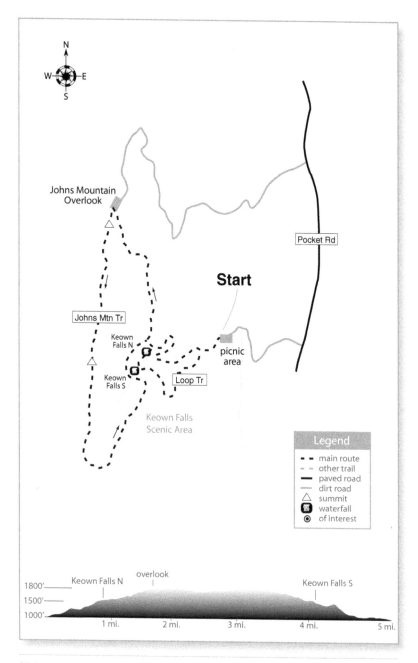

N
W E
S

Johns Mountain
Overlook

Pocket Rd

Start

Johns Mtn Tr

Keown
Falls N

picnic
area

Keown
Falls S

Loop Tr

Keown Falls
Scenic Area

Legend

- - main route
- - other trail
— paved road
— dirt road
△ summit
▨ waterfall
◉ of interest

overlook

Keown Falls N

Keown Falls S

1800'
1500'
1000'

1 mi.   2 mi.   3 mi.   4 mi.   5 mi.

🚶 House of Dreams Loop

Hike Distance	6.1 miles
Type of Hike	Loop
Difficulty	Moderate
Hiking Time	Half Day
Start Elevation	775 ft
Total Ascent	960 ft
Land Manager	Berry College
Fee	None

A storybook stone tower stands beside Berry College's House of Dreams.

Martha Berry had a big dream in 1902—to start a school for mountain children. Starting in a one-room school house called Possum Trot, her dream has grown into a full-fledged college with a campus of almost 30,000 acres—the largest college campus in the world. Atop Lavender Mountain, high above the college, sits Miss Berry's House of Dreams. It's a wonderful wood and stone building that even today inspires people to dream big. Looking out over the Oostanaula River Valley, you can see for miles, right from the flower-covered front lawn.

This hike begins beside the Old Mill on the college's Mountain Campus. You'll hike up to the House of Dreams, first on a trail through an experimental longleaf pine plantation, then on gated dirt roads. After you reach the summit and view the house, a foot trail takes you along the spine of the mountain toward a high lake which holds the college's water supply. From there you'll again walk along pleasant, gated dirt roads, then back through the pines to the Old Mill.

Getting to the Trailhead

Berry College is located in Mt. Berry just north of Rome, off US 27. Once on campus, follow the signs to the Mountain Campus and then to the Old Mill.

GPS Coordinates
N 34° 19.48' W 85° 14.98'

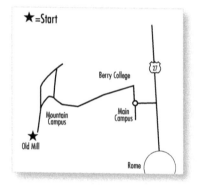

Hiking Directions

Begin Walk back down the road you drove in on.

Mile 0.2 Turn left onto Longleaf Trail.

Mile 0.6 Turn right on a dirt road which runs fairly level along the side of the mountain.

Mile 1.2 Turn left on the main dirt road that heads up and over Lavender Mountain.

Mile 1.9 Turn left through the arched gate leading to the House of Dreams.

Mile 2.8 Reach House of Dreams. Take some time to look around, then continue onto the foot trail on the far side.

Mile 4.2 Turn left on dirt road.

Mile 5.5 Close the loop by turning right down the Longleaf Trail. Retrace your route from here back to the trailhead.

Mile 6.1 Finish.

The route begins by the Old Mill. Its wheel is 42 feet high.

House of Dreams Loop Trail Map

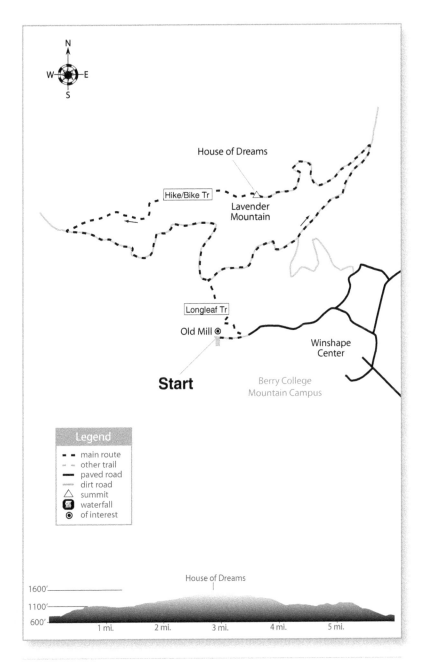

Northwest Georgia

Appendices

BENTON MacKAYE TRAIL ON RICH MOUNTAIN

Appendix A—Resources Contact Information

Chattahoochee National Forest (USFS)

Forest Supervisor's Office
Chattahoochee–Oconee National Forests
1755 Cleveland Hwy
Gainesville, GA 30501
770-297-3000
fs.usda.gov/conf

Armuchee–Cohutta Ranger District
3941 Hwy 76
Chatsworth, GA 30705
706-695-6736

Brasstown Ranger District
1881 Hwy 515
Blairsville, GA 30514
706-745-6928

Chattooga Ranger District
200 Hwy 197 N
Clarkesville, GA 30523
706-754-6221

Tallulah Ranger District
809 Hwy 441 South
Clayton, GA 30525
706-782-3320

Toccoa Ranger District
6050 Appalachian Hwy
Blue Ridge, GA 30513
706-632-3031

Georgia Department of Natural Resources

Web address for all parks:
GeorgiaStateParks.org

Georgia State Parks
1352 Floyd Tower East
2 Martin Luther King Dr
Atlanta, GA 30334
800-864-7275

Amicalola Falls State Park
418 Amicalola Falls State Park Rd
Dawsonville, GA 30534
706-265-4703

Black Rock Mountain State Park
3085 Black Rock Mountain Pkwy
Mountain City, GA 30562
706-746-2141

Cloudland Canyon State Park
122 Cloudland Canyon
State Park Rd
Rising Fawn, GA 30738
706-657-4050

Fort Mountain State Park
181 Fort Mountain Park Rd
Chatsworth, GA 30705
706-422-1932

Tallulah Gorge State Park
PO Box 248
Tallulah Falls, GA 30573
706-754-7970

Vogel State Park
405 Vogel State Park Rd
Blairsville, GA 30512
706-745-2628

Georgia Department of Natural Resources–Wildlife Resources

Wildlife Resources Division State Headquarters
2070 US Hwy 278 SE
Social Circle, GA 30025
770-918-6400
gohuntgeorgia.com

Northwest Region Office
(Crockford–Pigeon Mountain Wildlife Management Area)
2592 Floyd Springs Rd
Armuchee, GA 30105
706-295-6041

Northeast Region Office (Dawson Forest Wildcat & Amicalola Tract)
2150 Dawsonville Hwy
Gainesville, GA 30501
770-535-5700

Berry College

2277 Martha Berry Hwy NW
Mt Berry, GA 30149
706-232-5374
berry.edu

Summit bagging? It's when you hike to the top of as many high peaks as you can. Some people try for the highest in every state or all those in the East above 6,000 feet. Others take it to extremes, for example, the highest on every continent—you get the idea. If you hike every route in this book, you'll bag a total of 31 summits, including the two highest in Georgia.

Summit	Page
Rabun Bald (#2)	30
Pinnacle Knob	33
Black Rock Mountain	36
Lookoff Mountain	39
Chenocetah Mountain	54
Brasstown Bald (#1)	65
Eagle Knob	77
Tray Mountain (#7)	83
Rocky Mountain	86
Mt. Yonah	89
Wildcat Mountain	99
Cowrock Mountain	101
Coosa Bald (#11)	107
Blood Mountain (#6)	110
Levelland Mountain	116
Sassafras Mountain	133
Brawley Mountain	136
Tooni Mountain	145
Rich Mountain	148
Springer Mountain	154
Frosty Mountain	160
Hickory Ridge	171
Grassy Mountain	177
Bald Mountain	180
Flat Top Mountain	186
Fowler Mountain	186
Fort Mountain	192
Pigeon Mountain	213
Taylors Ridge	219
Johns Mountain	222
Lavender Mountain	225

Georgia's Highest Summits

Brasstown Bald

1	Brasstown Bald	4,784 ft
2	Rabun Bald	4,698 ft
3	Dicks Knob	4,620 ft
4	Hightower Bald	4,568 ft
5	Wolfpen Ridge	4,561 ft
6	Blood Mountain	4,458 ft
7	Tray Mountain	4,430 ft
8	Grassy Ridge	4,420 ft
9	Slaughter Mountain	4,338 ft
10	Double Spring Knob	4,280 ft
11	Coosa Bald	4,280 ft

Appendix C—Hike Routes in State Parks

Amicalola Falls State Park

Amicalola Falls Loop 157
AT Approach Loop............. 160

Black Rock Mountain State Park

Tennessee Rock Trail............. 36
J.E. Edmonds Trail 39

Cloudland Canyon State Park

West Rim Loop................... 204
Sittons Gulch Trail 207

Fort Mountain State Park

Stone Tower Loop.............. 192
Cool Springs Loop.............. 195
West Face Loop................ 198

Tallulah Gorge State Park

Tallulah Gorge Circuit........... 48

Vogel State Park

Bear Hair Gap Trail 104
Coosa Backcountry Trail 107

Appendix D—Hike Routes on the Appalachian Trail

Route	Page
Whiteoak Stomp View.......... 42	
Chattahoochee Source 77	
Tray Mountain Summit........... 83	
Rocky Mountain Loop 86	
Whitley Gap Shelter 98	
Cowrock Mountain View...... 101	
Slaughter Creek Loop 110	
Blood Mountain Loop 113	
Levelland Mountain View...... 116	
Preaching Rock View 127	
Woody Gap Ramble 130	
Sassafras Mountain View 133	

Rich Mountain Loop 148
Long Creek Falls 151
Springer Mountain Loop...... 154

Appendix E—Hike Routes on the Bartram Trail

Route   **Page**

Rabun Bald Trail 30   Pinnacle Knob View 33

Appendix F—Hike Routes on the Benton MacKaye Trail

Route   **Page**

Brawley Mountain Firetower 136   Rich Mountain Loop 148
Deadennen Mountain View 139   Long Creek Falls 151
Wallalah Mountain View 142   Springer Mountain Loop...... 154
Toccoa River Bridge 145   Fowler Mountain View 186

Appendix G—Hike Routes with Waterfalls

Route   **Page**

Three Forks Trail 24   Amicalola Falls Loop 157
Holcomb Creek Trail 27   Wildcat Creek Trail 163
Pinnacle Knob View 33   Jacks River Falls 168
J.E. Edmonds Trail 39   Rice Camp Loop................. 171
Hemlock Falls Trail 45   Panther Creek Falls.............. 174
Tallulah Gorge Circuit........... 48   Panther Bluff View 183
Chenocetah Mountain 54   Emery Creek Trail............... 189
Nancytown Falls 57   Cool Springs Loop.............. 195
High Shoals Trail 80   West Face Loop 198
Dukes Creek Falls 92   Sittons Gulch Trail 207
Raven Cliffs Trail 95   High Point Loop.................. 213
Desoto Falls Trail................. 119   Rocktown Loop.................... 216
Dockery Lake Trail............... 124   Johns Mountain Loop.......... 222
Long Creek Falls 151

Milestone Press

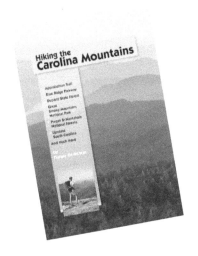

Hiking

- *Hiking the Carolina Mountains* by Danny Bernstein

- *Hiking North Carolina's Blue Ridge Mountains* by Danny Bernstein

- *Day Hiking the North Georgia Mountains* by Jim Parham

- *Waterfall Hikes of Upstate South Carolina* by Thomas E. King

- *Waterfall Hikes of North Georgia* by Jim Parham

- *Hiking Atlanta's Hidden Forests: Intown & Out* by Jonah McDonald

- *Backpacking Overnights: North Carolina Mountains South Carolina Upstate* by Jim Parham

- *Wildflower Walks & Hikes: North Carolina Mountains* by Jim Parham

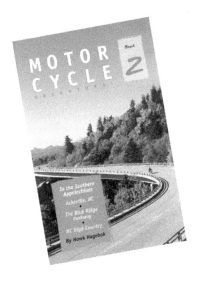

Motorcycle Adventures
by Hawk Hagebak

- *1–Southern Appalachians:*
  North GA, East TN,
  Western NC

- *2–Southern Appalachians:*
  Asheville NC,
  Blue Ridge Parkway,
  NC High Country

- *3–Central Appalachians:*
  Virginia's Blue Ridge,
  Shenandoah Valley,
  West Virginia Highlands

Mountain Biking
by Jim Parham

- *Mountain Bike Trails:*
  NC Mountains -
  SC Upstate

- *Mountain Bike Trails:*
  North GA - Southeast TN

Milestone Press

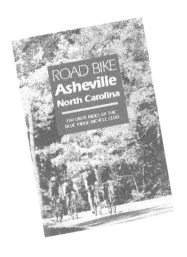

Road Bike Guide Series

- *Road Bike Asheville, NC: Favorite Rides of the Blue Ridge Bicycle Club* by The Blue Ridge Bicycle Club

- *Road Bike North Georgia: 25 Great Rides in the Mountains and Valleys of North Georgia* by Jim Parham

- *Road Bike the Smokies* by Jim Parham

Family Adventure

- *Natural Adventures in the Mountains of North Georgia* by Mary Ellen Hammond & Jim Parham

- *Family Hikes in Upstate South Carolina* by Scott Lynch

Pocket Guides

- *Hiking South Carolina's
  Foothills Trail*
  by Scott Lynch

- *Hiking & Mountain Biking
  Dupont State Forest*
  by Scott Lynch

- *Hiking & Mountain Biking
  Pisgah Forest*
  by Jim Parham

Milestone Press books can be found at your local bookseller
and/or outfitters, or you can visit our website, www.ugapress.org.
Phone orders can be placed by calling 800-848-6224.

Printed in the USA
CPSIA information can be obtained
at www.ICGtesting.com
LVHW061406021224
798086LV00005B/34